SPREADING THE GOSPEL

being
BOOK FOUR
of
BACKGROUND TO THE BIBLE

by

Bernard R. Youngman

(author, "Teaching Religious Knowledge")

HULTON EDUCATIONAL PUBLICATIONS

TO THOSE WHO READ THIS BOOK

THE recorded story of the Bible falls naturally into four parts: from Abraham to Solomon, from the Divided Kingdom to the Coming of Christ, the Life and Teaching of Christ, and the Spread of Christianity.

The books in this series follow this sequence:

    Book   I: Patriarchs, Judges and Kings.
    Book II: Prophets and Rulers.
    Book III: The Palestine of Jesus.
    Book IV: Spreading the Gospel.

What this book and the others in this series set out to do is to provide background information of all kinds about the Land and the People of the Bible, their lives, occupations, names, customs, beliefs, and so on. Lots of pictures—photographs and drawings—have been included to help you to "see" more vividly the events and experiences of these Bible people, in the hope that you will realise more clearly just what God meant to them in their days and what He might mean to you and me today.

Be sure to study the Bible passages given you in each chapter—that is something you must not fail to do.

First published 1956

Second Impression 1957

Reprinted 1958

Reprinted 1959

Reprinted 1960

Reprinted 1961

Reprinted 1963

HULTON EDUCATIONAL PUBLICATIONS, 55 Saffron Hill, London, E.C.1.
Made and printed in Great Britain by William Clowes and Sons, Limited, London and Beccles

CONTENTS

ACKNOWLEDGMENTS

Grateful acknowledgments are made to the following for the use of copyright photographs :

Shell Photographic Unit, Eric Deuchars, A. F. Kersting, The Mansell Collection, Picture Post Library, Paul Popper Ltd., Exclusive News Agency Ltd., J. Allan Cash, Donald McLeish, The British Museum, Central Press Photos Ltd., Charles E. Brown, G. H. Pritchard, The Greek Information Office, Keystone Press Agency, Rev. R. Clements, T. W. Dickenson, J. C. Rogerson, Fox Photos Ltd.

The drawings were prepared by Y. M. Poulton, Pierre Savoie and Michael Ford to whom thanks are also due.

INTRODUCTION

THE BOOK OF THE ACTS is sometimes called "the Gospel of the Holy Spirit". What this means we shall find in this book. The narrative falls into two almost equal parts. The first fifteen chapters tell the story of the Christian Church during its earliest years, how it began and how Jews and Gentiles (non-Jews) were united in the new Christian faith. The remaining twelve chapters tell the story of Paul, whose missionary tours spread the newly begun Christian Church throughout the Roman Empire.

The *Acts* is a history book, an adventure story, a book of plots and intrigues; it is a biography, a book to stir, to challenge and to study. Its hero is Christ, but the chief character is Paul, working in the power of the Holy Spirit.

The last paragraph of Book III told how the disciples, happy in the knowledge that their Lord had gone "to prepare a place for them" and was ever present with them, went to the Upper Room to await the gift of the powerful Holy Spirit that had been promised by Jesus. At Pentecost the Christian Church was born. *Acts* continues this story. It appears to have been written about A.D. 82.

Who wrote the Book of the *Acts*? There seems little doubt in the minds of men who make it their life work to study such matters—we call them New Testament scholars—that the author was Luke. Remember that Luke was *not* a disciple of Jesus, although he wrote the Gospel bearing his name and telling about the life and work of the Master. Luke was, in fact, a Greek doctor, probably from Philippi, and a Christian. He first met Paul at Troas and from that time became his loyal friend and great admirer. Both men were well educated and cultured, and must have found much pleasure in each other's company for conversation and exchange of ideas:

they spent a great deal of time together, for Luke went with Paul on his travels, looking after him not only as a friend but also as a doctor, for Paul was often in need of treatment for illnesses and severe pain. You will find references to Luke in Col. iv, 12; 2 Tim. iv, 11; Phile. 24. *Acts* contains first-hand or what we call "eye-witness" accounts of certain incidents at which we know Luke was present. These are the "we" passages. You can find them in xvi, 10–17; xx, 5–15; xxi, 1–17; xxvii, 1– xviii, 18.

Knowing that Luke was so close a friend to Paul, we expect something of Paul's tremendous enthusiasm, zeal and sense of adventure to become real and clear in the narrative. This is exactly what happens and no one can deny that Paul as a man "comes alive" in the story in such a way that the writer must have been someone who knew him better than anyone else.

Those who have made a study of such matters tell us that Luke wrote the *Acts* as well as the Gospel that bears his name. They have found that:

i. Both the *Acts* and the *Gospel of St. Luke* are dedicated to the same person, a Greek friend of noble birth named Theophilus (Luke i, 1–4; Acts i, 1).

ii. The style in *Luke* and the *Acts* is much the same. This is easier to tell by scholars who can read the original Greek in which the two books were written.

iii. There are medical words and phrases which fit in with the idea that Luke was a doctor (iii, 7; viii, 7; ix, 18; xviii, 13). Notice these and others in your reading.

The *Acts* reveals Paul's desire that the Christian Church should be a united body of people, where there was joyous friendship and brotherhood and a tremendous urge to share their love and happiness with one another in the belief that Jesus, their Lord and Master, was living with them, united to them by the wonderful power of the Holy Spirit.

And what about Luke himself? From his writings he seems to have been a kindly, sympathetic man, gentle and patient, modest and quietly critical—just the kind of person who makes a good doctor. He was a careful writer, too, and made it his business to be exact in his descriptions. A great archaeologist, Sir William Ramsay, has said that Luke's information is historically correct and trustworthy. Many of the references once misunderstood or contradicted by earlier scholars translating his writings have now been found to be accurate. Much of

his work was, of course, from his own experience of what Paul was doing. Paul's friends also told him about the growing Church and sent reports to Luke; and it is probable that here and there Luke collected some written information about the early beginnings of the Christian faith of which he had no first-hand knowledge himself.

Luke set himself a difficult task when he wrote the *Acts*. He chose incidents that covered the work of the apostles and Paul, and told them in a wonderfully vivid way. Some people think that he planned yet a third book, for this one ends rather abruptly. But we are grateful to him for this story that tells how the Church began and how Paul continued it. That story is only the beginning of Christianity, for it has gone on right up to this very moment.

BACKGROUND TO THE ACTS

IN order to understand the story of the growth and spread of Christianity we need to be clear about its background. The then known world was the Roman Empire (see map), encircling the Great (Mediterranean) Sea, reaching "from the Tyne to the Euphrates", with Italy at its centre and Rome at its heart. Palestine was but a very small part. Look at the map and see just how small it was. As we saw in Book III, Chapter 1, there were three main peoples of the world—the Greeks, the Romans and the Jews, each of whom in different ways had important influences upon the empire, its divisions, its religions and its cultures.

The Greeks

The Greeks, under Alexander the Great, had swept through Asia Minor, Palestine and the East, taking with them wherever they had gone the culture, art and beauty of their own land. Long after the fall of their empire (to the Romans) their architecture, poetry, philosophy and art in many forms had left their mark, and it is for these that today we remember the Greeks. Of even greater importance, however, was their language. Conquered nations found it easy to read, learn and speak, and it became the chief language of the whole empire and the nations within it. This enabled peoples of countries far apart to understand one another, to trade and to exchange ideas; it became the means of spreading by word of mouth and by written letters the Good News of the Christian Faith. The New Testament was written in Greek, and the Septuagint (LXX) translation of the Old Testament (Book II, Chapter 11) was read in all synagogues throughout the empire.

When this empire was taken over by the Romans they could not conquer the wonderful influence of Greek culture. They could not make the peoples speak the Roman tongue—Latin. All over the empire there remained Greek colonies; some of them included Jews who had accepted the Greek or Hellenist ways of living and were known as Hellenist Jews. In Decapolis (ten cities) to the east of the Jordan there were Greek towns in the time of Jesus. You will recall that He healed the madman in Decapolis. Paul was to find many of these Greek communities in his travels westwards.

The Romans

But when the Romans conquered nations they allowed them to a great extent to continue their religions, language and normal ways of living, so long as there were no rebellions and disorders. Thus, the Herods were allowed to rule in Palestine under the power of Rome, and the High Priest had religious and civil control over the Jews in Jerusalem. The only reason Pilate was there as Governor (Procurator) was that the Jews of Judaea had rebelled against their own ruler Archelaus and had asked for Roman control.

Rome brought peace—the Pax Romana—and enabled the empire to settle and progress. Roman forms of government were introduced, with courts of law and justice, and captive peoples ruled themselves by these. In the chief cities were "planted" colonies of Romans. These were usually ex-service men, whose presence tended to prevent uprisings and riots, for they could quickly band together to check disorders. Do not forget that it was at this time that England was part of the Roman Empire, and here, too, the Roman settlers were colonies of ex-service men. Of course, the invading armies brought back to Rome thousands of slaves; these were bought and sold like cattle, and put to work on building huge arenas and amphitheatres. You will remember that Jesus was but a lad when the Galileans rebelled; many were crucified and thousands were sent from their homes in lovely Galilee to pagan Rome. Rome taxed the people, too. In Book III we found what a great burden upon the Jews this taxation really was.

Ploughing in Galilee. These fields were tilled in the days of the Romans, with the same care and with similar ploughs and oxen.

Roman rule was powerful and firm. Roman armies were well trained and well equipped and were stationed in camps and garrisons throughout the empire. One important garrison was even in Jerusalem. The Castle of Antonia (named in honour of the Roman Antony) was a stronghold overlooking the Temple itself. It was necessary, especially during festivals, to keep an eye on possible uprisings and anti-Rome demonstrations. This garrison saved Paul from the angry Jews, as we shall see.

Through her armies Rome became absolute mistress of her vast empire. Yet there was great pride in being a Roman citizen. Freedom, even from slavery, could be bought or earned by some valuable service.

But the Romans were brutal and pagan. Their gods and goddesses—Venus, Jupiter, Diana, Mars, Bacchus, Mithras . . . were worshipped in fear and superstition, satisfied only with sacrifices and evil rituals. These gods ruled everything they did, and it is not surprising that the people found their lives empty and meaningless and themselves lonely and afraid. Such an empire, without love and goodness and a religion of noble worship, could not last—and as history

Bedouin and their tents.

Jerusalem today. A mosque occupies the Temple site.

Life in the market where goods are bought and sold, news is exchanged and rumours are spread.

shows, it did not. Yet it was at the height of its cruel power when the Christian Church was just beginning and spreading.

The Jews

It is important to remember that the Jews had spread throughout the Mediterranean lands long before the persecutions of the early Church. Indeed, we have to go back as far as the time of the Babylonian conquest (Book II, Chapter 9) and no doubt there were scattered groups even before that. These were the Jews of the Dispersion (Diaspora). Some of the places in which they had settled are given in Acts ii, 9–11. They had settled in the main cities as traders, fugitives, even as slaves. There they had lived their Jewish lives but obviously not without some influence from the people amongst whom they lived. They spoke Greek as well as their own Aramaic or Hebrew tongue, used the Greek Septuagint as well as their precious Hebrew scrolls and wore Greek dress and clothes. They even changed their Jewish names to Greek and Roman forms, and had their meals in Greek or Roman fashion (Book III, p. 49).

But wherever they happened to be, usually in colonies of the great cities, they managed to keep their own faith amidst the wickedness and cruelty of false idol worship, superstition, witchcraft and sorcery. They kept their belief in Yahweh, the One True God. Wherever there were ten males

they could form a synagogue, and this they did. They maintained their rites and ceremonies and kept themselves as free from the "unclean" Gentiles as they possibly could.

An old Syrian merchant.

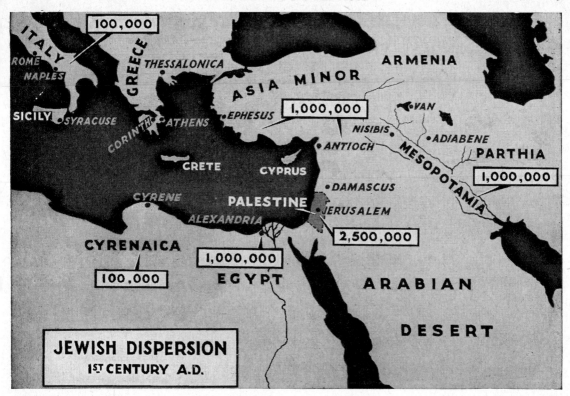

JEWISH DISPERSION
1ST CENTURY A.D.

This map gives us some idea of the numbers of Jews outside Palestine at this time.   Wherever there were even ten males they set up a synagogue for their worship.

The Temple was their "home" and every year thousands of Jews made their way to Jerusalem as a sacred duty. The most devout Jews, as we should expect, lived in Jerusalem. At a time when many Greeks and Romans were growing tired of their gods and the uselessness of their worship, weary of the vice and wickedness of the emperor's court and anxious at the low standards of behaviour of the people, some found in the Jewish religion what they were seeking—a belief in a single God whose power enabled men and women to be true to their faith and live clean lives. It seemed to be a satisfying religion when compared with their own. These non-Jews joined the synagogue and obeyed sufficient of the Jewish Law to be accepted in worship. They were called "proselytes" or God-fearers. They paid their synagogue dues and religious taxes but did not become full Jews.

Of course, in their blind narrow following of the Law of Moses and the many rites and regula-tions springing from it called the Tradition, the strict Jews often made their religion a burden-some keeping of rules. Jesus had had many a quarrel with them over such matters (Book III). They denied and rejected Jesus and crucified their Messiah, and then refused to believe that He was the One for Whom they had waited. These strict Jews were enemies of the Christian belief in the Risen Christ. Those Palestinian Jews who did accept Him were also anxious to keep their Jewish ways; they were to find that they could not serve both faiths at once. It was left to the Hellenist Jews with their freer and wider beliefs to welcome the Good News and to give the first preachers and missionaries the help and encouragement needed to spread the new faith.

The Jews and Christianity

When the split came in the main Jewish reli-gion, these Hellenist Jews were ready to pass over the old strict Laws and Judaism in order to

Athens as it appeared to Paul. The Parthenon crowns the Acropolis; in the fine colonnaded buildings Greek art, culture and philosophy were taught.

accept the new universal faith of Christianity. The Palestinian Jews were rather more nervous of doing so. But the Hellenists argued that Judaism was for the Jews only, whereas Christianity was for everybody. The Gospel broke down all barriers. Jerusalem had always been "off the map", away from the important trade and caravan routes linking Egypt through Palestine with Asia Minor and the countries to the north-east. It was therefore little touched by the great movement of Christianity which would appeal to the non-Jews elsewhere. That is why—despite the first believers under Peter—Christianity did not centre in Jerusalem. It really developed in Syria, among the non-Jews and proselytes of Antioch. Here were laid the foundations of the Christian world church whose members included Jews, Gentiles, Samaritans, free citizens and slaves, rich and poor, learned and ignorant, scholars, philosophers, sorcerers, soldiers. Through Christ had come a man who was neither Jew nor Gentile; he was a Christian. It was Paul who brought Christianity to the Gentiles and enabled them to see that all divisions were broken down, for there were no barriers between Christians (Gal. iii, 28). He shook off the shackles of Jewish ceremonies and rituals that Jesus had so firmly denounced throughout His Ministry (Book III).

Thus it was that each of these three great nations had much to give—the Greeks their language and culture so that everyone could hear and understand the Good News; the Romans their strong control of different peoples,

their discipline, their fine roads whereby the News could travel, the peace which enabled the Christian missionaries to continue their work without the interference of wars; the Jews, with their strong belief in the One True God, their longing for their Messiah and their desire to be

The old and the new. Along the Appian Way.

Nomadic women still work at their primitive craft; weaving as it has been done through the centuries.

His chosen people. To these three great nations came Christianity, free from the chains of Judaism, challenging the pagan worship of Greece and Rome, bringing people of all nations into a brotherhood that mere empires have never before or since believed possible.

A fine statue of a Roman ruler of this period.

EXPRESSION WORK

1. "The Book of the *Acts* is sometimes called the Gospel of the Holy Spirit." What do you think is the meaning of this?
2. How do we know that Luke wrote the *Acts*? Prepare notes for a talk to the class on this.
3. From information and references in this book, together with further help from Commentaries, write a biography of Luke.
4. Find references in the *Gospel of St. Luke* and the *Acts* that show Luke's special knowledge of or interest in medical matters.
5. As Luke, interview some of Paul's friends for information about Paul and the Early Church.
6. Write to John Mark for information about himself, Barnabas and Paul.
7. The "new church" is marked by its Fellowship, Love and Boldness. Find quotations in Acts i–v to illustrate these aspects.
8. Let a Greek, a Roman and a Jew discuss the "new religion".
9. What was the Septuagint (LXX)? How was it made?
10. List eight Roman gods and goddesses. Find their Greek names. Say for what each was worshipped.
11. Why were there so many Jews in the great cities of the Roman Empire? Why was their presence likely (*a*) to help, (*b*) to hinder, Paul in his work?
12. Who were the "proselytes"? Why were the Jews jealous of Paul's preaching as far as these people were concerned?

CHAPTER 2

PENTECOST

(Luke xxiv, 50–53; Acts i)

The Ascension

READ again the wonderful account of the Resurrection in John xx, 1–8, and Luke xxiv, 1–11.

During the Forty Days from His Resurrection, as His rising from the dead on Easter Sunday is called, Jesus had appeared nine times to His disciples, when they were feeling sad and uncertain about their belief in Him. Because of His appearance they had come to see that He was still alive and that, although in future they could not see Him as they had done when He was living with them, He would be near them all the time. It was this certainty of His being near to them that made such a great difference to them. Gradually they changed from being frightened, doubting and anxious followers to brave, confident and outspoken preachers of His Gospel—the Good News about their Master. This Good News was that Jesus, the promised Messiah, had risen from the dead and was alive and would come again soon to take charge of their lives. As Jews they had always believed that the Messiah had chosen them as His own people, and this thought was still very much in their minds. God had proved that He was powerful over everything, even death itself, which with sin and wickedness was now conquered.

They expected Jesus to return quickly, and stories of the early days of their meetings and lives show that they were in readiness. It was only as time went on that they realised that God, as Jesus had said, would choose His own time. Meanwhile, they were to preach His Kingdom in Jerusalem, Judaea, Samaria and so throughout the world (Acts i, 6–8).

Jesus had promised His disciples the gift of the Holy Spirit—the Comforter. This word really means "strengthener"—one who gives power to overcome weakness. The Holy Spirit would come upon them, but now that they were sure of Him He must return to His Father. We call this return the *Ascension.*

Matthias is Elected

Still in the hope that Jesus would come soon, the disciples made their way back from the Mount of Olives, a sabbath day's journey of two thousand cubits (a cubit=18–20″). They went to the Upper Room or Chamber in Mark's mother's house in Jerusalem (xii, 12). This was where they had met on many occasions since the Last Supper and where they held their prayer meetings. As there were eleven of them as well as friends and followers of Jesus—including the brothers of Jesus and Mary herself—it is possible that they held services very much like those followed in the synagogue (vi, 4; xvi, 13). They joined "in gladness" (ii, 46), in the "breaking of bread and drinking of the cup" which reminded them of the Last Supper and fellowship with their Master (Luke xxiv, 43; Acts x, 41).

The twelfth disciple—the only Judaean, for all the others were from Galilee—had killed himself for having cruelly betrayed His Master. The story of his death in i, 16–20, is probably more accurate than that in Matt. xxvii, 3–10, but both should be read. It was now necessary to fill the place of Judas. Peter deliberately made the scriptures fit the facts—Ps. lxix, 25; cix, 8—as he explained the position to the others. They believed that the casting of lots would be guided by the decision of God. This was a common method of choosing; it was done for Temple duties amongst the priests.

Matthias, who had known Jesus and had seen His work, crucifixion and resurrection, was chosen. We do not hear of him again, but that is also true of several of the original disciples. *Acts* is only a partial account of the growth of the Church, and much is left unrecorded. It would be wrong to argue that because he is not

In an Upper Room like this the disciples met on the Day of Pentecost.

mentioned again Matthias was a failure. No doubt all the disciples in their various ways did important work in the building up of the new faith, for they had been "eye-witnesses" and knew what was meant by His Kingdom. We see that already the Twelve are a distinct set or group within the larger community; they may even have felt that twelve was a desirable number to correspond with the original twelve called by Jesus and possibly with the twelve tribes of Israel.

Pentecost

It was now May, A.D. 29, ten days after the last appearance of Jesus and fifty since Passover.

The time was therefore *Pentecost*, which means "fiftieth" or "week of weeks" (Lev. xxiii, 15–21). This was the ancient festival of the giving of the Law on Sinai (Ex. xix, 16–19). In time the festival had become linked with the early harvest of Syria (May and June) and was recognised as a Harvest Festival of First Fruits or Feast of Weeks (Ex. xxxiv, 22; xxiii, 16; Num. xxviii, 26). At this time worshippers brought to the Temple two loaves of bread (rather like pancakes, you will remember) made from the new corn, and the priests "waved" them before the altar. It was a time of rejoicing and thanks to God and was, of course, one of the great

The Mount of Olives as it is today. In the foreground is the Garden of Gethsemane.

The modern shepherd leads his sheep to pasture.

"Speaking with Tongues"

Filled with this new power and thrilled with a great sense of purpose, the disciples seem to have broken into "babblings". These were possibly repeated cries of praise. Even today at meetings where people are stirred deeply, like Negro prayer meetings, such sounds may be heard. Unable to express themselves in other ways the people, overflowing with excitement and emotion, cry out single words and phrases like "Praise to God" and "Hallelujah" (which means the same thing) or "Amen", until very often these are the only words that can be clearly heard at all. The charge made against the disciples was that they were drunk, and this shows that much of what they were saying was quite unintelligible to those who listened outside. But those who stood near and felt the same thrill of praise would recognise many of the exclamations and cries. It is hardly likely that the disciples were suddenly given the power to speak foreign languages; what is more likely is that they spoke in Aramaic, the local dialect, or in Greek which would be understood by everybody, including the pilgrim Jews of the Dispersion.

With the gift of the Spirit came the power and confidence so to speak that men of all nations, creeds and classes might be told the Good News.

By now, the disciples seem to have left the Upper Room, for they are in the midst of a "multitude". The countries listed in verses 9–11

festivals of the year. Jerusalem would be crowded with pilgrims, for they were commanded to attend the Temple for this celebration (Ex. xxiii, 17; Deut. xvi, 16). They came from as far away as Rome, Athens, Alexandria, Baghdad; in fact, if they lived within ninety days' journey of Jerusalem they were expected to attend.

So, on this "old" Day of Pentecost, the disciples were waiting, gathered in prayer. There was in each one of them a growing sense of certainty and a feeling of excited joy that overflowed in a surge of emotion and fervour which we call ecstasy (1 Sam. x, 10; 1 Chron. xii, 18). They suddenly felt that God's Holy Spirit had indeed come and that the power and energy of Jesus had entered into each one of them. They *knew* that He was with them; this was the proof of the risen and living Christ.

The wind and the forked tongues of fire cannot be "explained". Luke speaks of the sound *like* a mighty rushing wind and refers to the appearance *as of* cloven tongues of fire (see also Matt. iii, 11; Ezek. xxxvii, 9. In 1 Kings xix, 11–13, there is a note of surprise that God was *not* "in the wind or the fire"). This is picture language and probably means that the disciples sensed a strange movement as of wind and felt their spirits burn with something rich and strange. What is more important for us to remember is that they passed through a wonderful experience that made them changed men.

The donkey is still a common means of transport.

The Kedron Valley below Jerusalem, looking towards Jericho.

are really languages and give some idea of the wide sweep of the Greek-speaking Jews (Hellenists) and Jews throughout the Roman Empire. Judaea probably means here Palestine and Syria where Aramaic was spoken. Whatever the actual events we now see the disciples as inspired and uplifted and thoroughly convinced of their mission to establish Christ's Kingdom. They felt freed from fear, from sin, from the power of evil and death. They were filled with a joy and an exuberance that were infectious and exciting.

Peter's Speech

Peter had already established himself as the leader of the company who formed the beginnings of the Christian Faith. We cannot imagine any other disciple taking his place although, as he and others of the Twelve moved from Jerusalem into the "uttermost parts", we find James the brother of Jesus taking charge of the early Church in Jerusalem. But with his usual bluntness and impetuosity, Peter takes up the challenge of the watchers. The first thing he has to deny is that they are drunk. It is but the third hour of the day, nine a.m. Morning prayers have not yet been said and wine is never taken before then. What they have seen, says Peter, is pro-

phecy being fulfilled—the sign of the day of Yahweh, promised by Joel (ii, 28–32). God's people were to be inspired and the heavens would show forth wondrous things. The first of these two signs is clear to see. It is the gift of the Holy Spirit, once seen in the prophets of old and now returned to all believers in the Messiah Who had descended from David. The second part—"the great and terrible day of the Lord"—is to come. This is to be the Messiah's Kingdom, already begun by Jesus. He was the Man Who had suffered, Whom the Jews had crucified and Whom they—the disciples—not only knew to be alive but would preach as Lord.

Note that Peter concentrates on the resurrection of Jesus as he addresses the people of Judaea who certainly knew of the ministry of Jesus. Some of the pilgrims knew, too. The whole Jewish nation had sinned and must repent. John the Baptist and other prophets had used baptism as the sign of acceptance of a new belief, of conversion. Now Peter says those who repented and believed must be baptised. It would be the outward sign of change from disbelief and doubt and evil living to a happy belief in Jesus as the risen Messiah and Lord of the new Kingdom (John i, 25). Sins would be forgiven and the gift of the inspiration of the Holy Spirit (sometimes called the Holy Ghost) would be theirs. In other words, there would now be the inner baptism of the Holy Spirit as well as the outer baptism of water.

The Nazarenes

Many of Peter's hearers had known Jesus well and were ready for this call; this is why the first converts, as they are called, were in such large numbers. At present they were called people "of the Way" (of the Way of Christ, that is) or "Nazarenes". It was not until later, as we shall see, that they were called Christians, although we use the word even as early as this. Pentecost was the birthday of the Christian Church. The word "church", of course, does not mean a building; it means a group or company of people.

Street trading in Jerusalem. What is being sold?

Acts ii, 42, shows that its members shared their goods and possessions, lived joyfully and were "ridiculously happy" in the belief that Jesus would suddenly return and set up His Kingdom. Worldly possessions were now useless for the heavenly Kingdom was theirs. It has been said that "Christian belief and Christian practice were two sides of the same coin" (Gal. v, 22) and that these people certainly "practised what they preached!" They still kept to their ordinary Jewish worship in the synagogues and at the Temple. Their main difference was their belief that the Messiah *had* come; other Jews were still expecting Him. They observed the Jewish sabbath (our Saturday) as a day of rest. But they also observed the first day of the week (our Sunday) with an early Communion or service of prayer and remembrance of the Lord's Resurrection. When, under Emperor Constantine, the Christians finally broke away from the Jewish faith, they also gave up the Jewish sabbath and kept Sunday as the Christian day of rest.

The larger the number of converts the more difficult became the problems of sharing (Gal. ii, 10; Acts xxiv, 17). Yet there was a wonderful sense of brotherhood amongst them and they joined "in prayer and breaking of bread". As yet, there were no Gentiles in the Church; upon these watchers "fear came". The word "fear" means "amazement and awe" rather than "being afraid". These watchers, the proselytes, were more than interested in the new strange religion which asserted that the Messiah had in fact come, had been killed by these very Jews, but was alive again. This was a remarkable teaching. These Gentiles had not been fully accepted by the Jews for full membership of their faith unless they also accepted all the rites and ceremonies demanded by the Jews for full membership. Now the proselytes wanted to be accepted by the Nazarenes—and what would be their answer? We shall see how this problem developed and how it was solved; for it led to the making of a tremendous decision—whether the new faith should remain Jewish or break away and become universal.

During the spread of Christianity the rite of baptism continued and, years later, this Jewish Festival was marked by all English Christians as a time of purity. They wore white and the day was known as White-Sunday-Tide or Whit-suntide, which is the name we use to this day.

Pharisees and Sadducees

These two groups of Jews have been mentioned many times in Books II and III. The Pharisees were strict Jews who believed that all that was necessary for good living was the keeping of the Law and hundreds of petty rules and regulations connected with it. The Sadducees, mostly of high-priestly families, wealthy and arrogant, were in the main the leaders of the Jewish Council, the Sanhedrin. They hated and despised the Phari-sees; they had no belief in life after death. But both sects were anxious about the spread of the new teaching of the disciples—the Pharisees be-cause it was being said that they were responsible for the death of Jesus, and the Sadducees because they did not accept the resurrection. In any case, to preach Christ as Messiah or King was to offend Rome and this would inevitably bring trouble. Both groups had thought that the cruci-fying of Jesus had put a stop to His work; but here were His disciples openly and boldly defying them and claiming that this "criminal" was alive. What was more serious was their claim that the Sanhedrin had murdered their own promised Messiah. If such a belief spread it would mean that the power the Pharisees and Sadducees held over the "common people" would be gone. It was this fear that had urged them to get rid of Jesus; now they had to deal with His disciples.

EXPRESSION WORK

1. Dr. Maltby has described the early Christ-ians as being "ridiculously happy". Was this true, do you think—and why?
2. Let Matthias and Joseph Barsabas chat to-gether (a) before, (b) after, the casting of the lots.
3. Look up the following references (and any others that you can find) on the Holy Spirit: Num. xi, 17; Num. xxvii, 18; Jud. iii, 10; Dan. v, 12; vi, 3; Matt. iii, 11; John iii, 5–8; xiv, 16–19, 25, 26; xv, 26, 27; xvi, 7–14.
4. Draw a map of the Mediterranean countries and show the districts mentioned in Acts ii. 9–11.

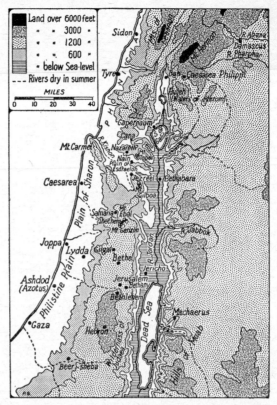

Palestine. Find on it the names of the places mentioned in the book.

5. Rewrite and declaim in modern speech Peter's first sermon.
6. Write and speak a dialogue between a strict and a Christian Jew.
7. What is the meaning of (a) the Ascension, (b) Whitsun?
8. Find all you can about the Pharisees and the Sadducees and say how and why they differed from the Christians.
9. Give three reasons why the early Christians should sell their possessions and share their money and goods.
10. Sketch Peter talking to the crowd.
11. As a Jew in Jerusalem, tell or write your friends about the events of Pentecost.
12. Who were the Nazarenes? Why were there as yet no Gentiles in the early church?
    or
    Letter for classroom display "O Lord, send into our hearts and the hearts of all men everywhere, the Spirit of Our Lord Jesus Christ."

CHAPTER 3

PETER AND JOHN

(iii; iv; v; vi, 1–7)

The Lame Man Healed

PETER and John kept their hours of worship as Jews, and went into the Temple Courts at the ninth hour—three p.m., the hour of the evening sacrifice. They were on the eastern side, at the Beautiful Gate (Nicanor) so called because it was cased in layers of gold and silver (Book II). Here the disciples saw the lame man who had his begging pitch at the gate. He expected "alms"—money—but Peter gave him his bodily health and strength. Note that the miracle was done "in the name of Jesus". We shall find this phrase much on the lips of Peter.

In Books II and III are descriptive references to the Temple. It was not a single large church as we know such a building, but rather a series of walled courts open to the sky and entered by special gates or from steps. Around the courts were cloisters or porches formed by pillars. In these cloisters Jesus had talked with the learned doctors of the Law and from the outer Court of the Gentiles, beyond which no Gentile could go on pain of death, He had cleared the money-changers and traders and animals. In the inner-most court stood the Temple itself, a small building with its Holy Place and Holy of Holies entered only by the High Priest. Sacrifices were offered on the rock altar and choirs of musicians (Levites) kept up their chants and praise whilst the sacrifices were held.

In Solomon's Porch or Cloister, outside the Temple itself, Peter spoke to the crowd that had gathered, and immediately connected the miracle with Jesus—whom the Jews had crucified, despite the willingness of the Gentile Pontius Pilate to release Him. But Jesus had risen from the dead and was their Messiah Who gave them the power to heal.

Needless to say the Sadducees, especially the High Priest Caiaphas, were "sore troubled", angry and anxious. Once again they were being faced with the challenge of the resurrection in which they did not believe. On their orders, the Captain of the Temple Guard arrested Peter and John on a charge of preaching the resurrection of the dead and especially of Jesus. The disciples were put into a cell until the next day when they would be questioned.

Meanwhile almost five thousand Jews, having seen or heard of the miracle of healing, accepted Peter's challenge and were baptised into the Church. Amongst them must have been many who a few weeks before had cried "Hosanna" on Palm Sunday; and there were others who had screamed their "Crucify Him!" These were now united as friends and brothers in their belief that Jesus was the risen Lord of them all.

Before the Sanhedrin

Peter and John faced the Sanhedrin, the Council of seventy and the High Priest who, under Rome, had the power to judge religious and civil matters amongst the Jews. The only thing they could not do was to carry out a death sentence, although they could recommend it to Rome. Annas had been deposed by Rome in favour of Caiaphas, his son-in-law; but he still held considerable power with the Jews. As far as Peter and John were concerned these priests had put their Master to death. The healed man was there, too, ready if need be to speak on their behalf. But Peter needed no help; he could speak for himself at any time. Urged by the Spirit he could speak for His Master, too. By what power and by what name had this man been healed? The Greek word for "power" contained a trap; it meant "magic"—which was against the law. Peter saw this and answered that his healing had been in the power of Jesus—Whom they had crucified and Who had risen from the dead. Jesus was the "head of the corner", said Peter. He was referring to the piece of stone that often

Even today the beggar has his "pitch".

money brought by the new converts. One of the first of the wealthy people to join was Joses Barnabas. His name means "Son of Consolation". He was a Greek Jew from Cyprus, and was to play an important part, as we shall see, in the growth of the early church.

In contrast is the story of Ananias and Sapphira. These two took advantage of the fact that Christians were sharing their goods, and by pretending to bring all their possessions were cheating their friends; at the same time they received praise for what appeared to be a noble act on their part. In this way they were mean and insincere towards God as well as towards their friends. Luke's account of what happened to them makes it appear that they were struck dead because they tried to deceive God. Some people accept this explanation. Others say that the shock of discovery of their cheating caused the death of Ananias, then the double shock of discovery and the death of her husband killed Sapphira. Such things have been known to happen.

lay hidden or neglected until the builders and masons wanted it, when it became the very piece —the key piece—needed to complete the building (Acts iv, 11; Ps. cxviii, 22).

The Sanhedrin were furious. They could not deny the miracle, for the healed man—whom they must have seen themselves very often—was there before them. But this talk of Jesus must stop. They realised that Peter and John, uneducated fishermen though they were, had a strange power of speech; they remembered, too, that these same men "had been with Jesus" Whose influence—if they dared to admit it— seemed to have given these men a quality that more than made up for any lack of learning.

All they could now do was to release them with a warning not to continue their preaching. Perhaps they hoped that an order from the chief Council would be sufficient. But they did not expect Peter's reply—Do we obey God—or you? And the Sanhedrin was defeated, for the time being.

Organising the Church

The disciples returned to their friends and their work, organising the pooling of goods and

Children play in an old tunnelled street.

The centuries slip away in this street.

"Cut to the heart", but afraid that the people would seek revenge upon them for the death of Jesus, the Sanhedrin determined to kill Peter and John, to prevent further preaching. But one of their number was a respected rabbi, a Doctor of the Law and a Pharisee; his name was Gamaliel. After Peter and John had been removed Gamaliel warned the Council not to be over-hasty in their actions. Other false prophets had arisen and had failed. If these disciples were false, said Gamaliel, they too would fail. But if they were genuinely of God, the Sanhedrin could do nothing to stop them; they could not fight "against God".

Peter and John were therefore beaten and warned again not to preach about Jesus. But as we should guess, they went straight to the Temple and continued their work fearlessly (Matt. v, 10). The Sadducees were anxious that nothing should create riots and disorders either from their own actions or from the preachings of the disciples. If Rome disapproved it would mean harsh interference and a possible end to their wealth and luxurious ways of living. They knew, too, that only a political charge such as treason could result in Rome's approval of the death sentence.

Before the Sanhedrin Again

It could not be long before the Sanhedrin again took action. Peter and John were flouting their warning and this time were thrown into prison. Next morning an amazed guard found the cell empty and reported to the alarmed Sanhedrin. Then came another report—the men were still preaching in the Temple Courts! This was incredible news to the pompous Council. Brought once more to the Chamber—without force or fuss so as not to attract the people's attention—Peter and John heard Caiaphas accuse them of stirring up strife and plotting revenge against the priests for the death of Jesus. The disciples gave their same answer, that they would "obey God rather than men". The Sanhedrin had crucified Jesus Who had risen again and of Whose life and work they, the disciples, had been witnesses and through Whom they had received the power of the Holy Spirit.

"I know My sheep and am known of Mine . . ."

The Pharisees and scribes were not so anxious. They did believe in the resurrection but were less concerned with the displeasure of Rome. Their main interest was in the Law and its Tradition which Jesus Himself had attacked but which so far had not been challenged by the disciples. They and the disciples believed in a Messiah; the only difference at the moment was that they did not believe in the same Messiah —Jesus.

The Seven Deacons

Meanwhile there was trouble in the new community. The Greek-speaking Jewish Christians complained that the Palestinian members were not being fair in their distributions of the goods and that the Hellenist widows were being neglected. Peter and John made it clear that they must preach, not "serve tables"; it was decided that all the administrative duties should be done by a group or committee of seven helpers, all of them Hellenists. They had to be men of high ideals and great tact; they must have received the Holy Spirit and should the need arise be capable of preaching and teaching (Deut. xxxiv, 9). Stephen and Philip (not to be confused with the disciple Philip) were two of the seven. Seven was the Jewish sacred number (e.g. the menorah or seven-branched candlestick).

So, for a while at least, the church ran itself smoothly whilst Peter and John continued to preach successfully, even winning over many of the priests (Acts vi, 7; John xii, 42, 43).

EXPRESSION WORK

1. Tell the story of the healing of the lame man from the point of view of (a) the man, (b) a watcher, or (c) a member of the Sanhedrin.
2. Find all you can (use Books I–IV of this series if possible) about the Temple. Prepare a talk for the class and make diagrams and drawings to illustrate what you have to say.
3. Dramatise "Peter and John before the Sanhedrin" (first occasion).
4. How was the Sanhedrin "defeated for the time being"?
5. As one of the Temple Guard, report verbally to the Sanhedrin the escape of the disciples from prison.
6. Prepare as a Dramatic Reading, v, 12–42. You will need a Narrator as well as individuals and groups to represent the main characters. This could be given in a Morning Assembly (see Qun. 11).
7. Write and act a play: i. The Sanhedrin assembles to try Peter and John. ii. The escape is reported (note verse 24). iii. Peter and John are charged. iv. They are released.
8. Why were the Sadducees especially interested in Peter and John?
9. Learn 1 Peter ii, 21–25. Letter for display verse 17.
10. Let Philip tell his daughters about the appointing of the seven "deacons", of whom he is one.
11. Prepare for Morning Assembly, a service on the theme "Serving God". Choose hymn, prayer and reading (see Qun. 6).
12. Interview Gamaliel.

This is a model of a synagogue such as the Jews built in the 1st Century A.D.

CHAPTER 4

STEPHEN, SAUL AND PHILIP

(vi, 8–15; vii; viii)

STEPHEN evidently attended the synagogues of the Hellenist Jews from Cilicia and district, and of the Jews from North Africa. (The word Libertines may mean "freedmen"—cf. liberty—but is more probably Libyans, of the same district as the other members.)

The members of the synagogues argued with Stephen who spoke with great wisdom and power. Obviously well-educated and of great faith in Jesus he even had the gift of healing. The Jews of his group and the Pharisees of the Jewish Law disputed with him about Jesus and found him a strong speaker. He was much more broad-minded than they and we shall see that there was a tendency for all Hellenist Jews to be readier in their beliefs about the new faith than were the stricter Jews of Jerusalem and Judaea.

His enemies became jealous as well as angry, for Stephen's arguments were beginning the rift between the new religion and Judaism that was to widen through the years and end in complete break-away from the Jewish faith. As so often in Jewish history, jealousy gave way to direct plotting, and false witnesses were bribed to accuse Stephen of speaking against God, that is, they laid a charge of blasphemy. The penalty for this was death by stoning (Lev. xxiv, 16). The Pharisees were now in league with the Sadducees against the new religion. They had banded together once before—to take action against Jesus.

Stephen's Defence

Stephen was brought before the Sanhedrin and stood in the same spot occupied by Peter a short time before. The Council sat in a wide semi-circle, the High Priest in the centre; at each end was a scribe noting evidence—one for, the other against, the prisoner. There were younger scribes and students of the Law seated on benches in front; perhaps Saul was among these. Most prisoners would have been overawed and frightened. Not so Peter; not so Stephen. His judges saw that his face was "as it had been the face of an angel". Despite their disbelief in angels, even the Sadducees were impressed by what they saw.

Stephen's speech made it clear that he believed that the new Law of Jesus was about to take the place of the old Law of Moses. He traced the history of the Jews from its beginnings to the time of Solomon who had built the first Temple. Up to this point his hearers listened intently. But Stephen went on to weave into that history the idea that the Law, the land and the Temple were not all-important but that other things came first! God had no need of a Temple made with hands; He could be anywhere. This, to the Sanhedrin, was blasphemy, an attack on their sacred Temple. They grew restless and angry. Stephen then went on to trace the Jewish persecutions of their own prophets, the very men who had prophesied the coming of the Messiah—the Just One. The Messiah had come and they—the Sanhedrin—had done exactly as their forefathers. They had rejected and killed Him and resisted the Holy Spirit. They had failed in their high duties and responsibilities. Now, Old Israel—Judaism—was passing; the New Israel—Christianity—had come in.

With his powerful words Stephen hammered in the wedge, deepening and widening the rift he had already made by his preaching. The Council seethed. They were again "cut to the heart" and like animals "gnashed their teeth upon him". Regardless, Stephen raised his eyes and seemed to see Jesus—not sitting at the right hand of God, but standing as though waiting to welcome him. As he told them of his vision the maddened judges rose at him, thrust him outside the city walls (1 Kings xxi, 13) to the ravine called the Place of Stoning, and there killed him. The false witnesses threw, as was their right, the first and

An artist's impression of Jews making their way to the synagogue.

sharpest jagged stones on which they could lay their hands (Deut. xvii, 17). This was mob law. The Roman garrison for once was too slow to act.

Stephen's dying words were those of his Master—"Lay not this sin to their charge" (Luke xxiii, 34). So, in A.D. 32 "fell asleep" Stephen, the first Christian martyr.

Amongst the watchers, protecting the clothes of those throwing the stones and therefore every bit as guilty of murder as they, was Saul of Tarsus, satisfied that this man was receiving the kind of death he deserved. Little did he know that, a few years later, he would tell the whole world that this was something he would never forget. Little did he dream that one day he, Saul, would continue the work of Stephen and widen this first rift with Judaism into a complete breakaway from the faith. For, as St. Augustine said, "We owe Paul to the prayer of Stephen."

Saul of Tarsus

Now that we have met the man who was to become the hero of our book it would be as well to know something more about him. Then we shall understand better why and how he felt about some things and acted in the ways that he did. Luke says that Saul was a young man. This would mean that he was about 30 years of age. He was born at Tarsus, "no mean city" of Cilicia (see map). The city stood a few miles from the coast on the river Cydnus, up which many years before in 41 B.C. the famous Egyptian Queen Cleopatra had sailed in her golden barge to meet Mark Antony. Perhaps Saul had heard of this from his father. The city itself had been established as a Greek capital by Antiochus Epiphanes (Book II) in 175–164 B.C. and many Jews lived there, too. In 64 B.C. Pompey, the Roman conqueror, had occupied it and made it a Roman colony, introducing Roman citizenship

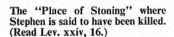

The "Place of Stoning" where Stephen is said to have been killed. (Read Lev. xxiv, 16.)

St. Stephen's Gate as it is today.

for Roman galleys and buildings. To the north of the city reared the Taurus Mountains, slashed through by the Cilician Gates, a narrow pass between mighty cliffs and frightening precipices. Here lurked panthers, bears and wolves, and here waited brigands and robbers. Famous in history, the pass was threaded by Cyrus and his Immortals on their way to Babylon in 401 B.C. and by Alexander the Great in 333 B.C. It was the way for the trading camel caravans from the north where lay the plateau of Asia Minor; so, came silks from China, ivory from India, carpets and spices from Persia, pottery from Syria, fish from Galilee, fruits from Damascus. These would be eagerly bartered in Tarsus market-place for goods arriving by sea—corn from Egypt, marble from Italy, glass from Sidon, copper from Cyprus, cedar from Joppa, pottery from Tuscany. In the market, too, would be the signs of the local industry. Goats were reared on the hill-slopes for their coarse black hair; this was woven into tents, sails, sacks and baling cloths, as well as into tough tunics and jackets and cloaks for protection against wind and weather (2 Tim. iv, 13).

Saul's Upbringing

Saul (that was his Jewish name) must have spent hours of his boyhood, as Jesus had done,

which Saul's father in some unknown way had managed to obtain; he may have bought it or earned it by some special service to Rome.

Tarsus

Tarsus was renowned for its learning, and its "University" was equal to those of Athens, Alexandria and Antioch. The university was not a building or group of colleges as we know Oxford or Cambridge; it was rather a centre of education where great and learned men, scholars, philosophers and teachers, gathered to discuss and teach and train their students. The Stoic philosophers, especially, with whom Paul was to talk in Athens years later, were well-known in Tarsus.

Around the city on the foothills of the northern mountains stretched great pine forests, and Tarsus became a famous timber city supplying wood

Paul as he was shown in the Catacombs.

The present gateway to Tarsus (Acts xxi, 39).

bermen, the brown sailors from Egypt, the hook-nosed Phoenicians, sallow Italians and dark Spaniards. He heard tales of the sea and the forests, sailed in and around the harbour and climbed into the pine woods. He listened to the gossip and rumours of traders, picking up their signs and accents and trading slang—a mixture of their own tongues and Greek. Like Amos and Jesus, though with no idea as to why, he noticed the cheating and dishonesty, and learned to distinguish between the honest man and the rogue.

In the city there was a Greek gymnasium where Saul watched athletes run and wrestle and play games (Eph. vi, 12; I Cor. ix, 24–27). Years later when he wanted to indicate what he had done with his life he spoke of having "fought the good fight" and "run his course" (2 Tim. iv. 7, 8; Phil. iii, 12–16). Although he was a Jew he was familiar with Greek customs, habits, forms of worship, and was able to recognise the statues and images of their gods and goddesses.

Saul's parents were apparently well-to-do. Their home was in the Jewish quarter of Tarsus. Although a strict Pharisee of the tribe of Benjamin, the smallest of the tribes, Saul was a Roman citizen. This he regarded as something of which to be very proud (Acts xxii, 27, 28; Phil. iii, 5; 2 Cor. xi, 22; Rom. ix, 3). It was to

watching and learning about people in the market-place and busy streets. By the quayside, docks and warehouses, he talked with the weather-beaten fishermen and sun-tanned lum-

Snowcapped, the Taurus Mts. rear formidably north of Tarsus.

Weaving was the local industry in Tarsus.

Receiving the "crown of laurels", the victor's reward.

serve him in good stead, as we shall see. He went to the synagogue school and as a "Hebrew of the Hebrews" from the time he could begin to learn he was trained in the sacred scriptures, the stories of his nation learned by Jesus and all Jewish boys. Saul wore his praying "talith" when, at 13, as a "son in the Law" he strapped on his phylacteries and worshipped in the synagogue. He learned his many texts and learned them well (Acts ix, 22). In his recorded speeches he referred to nearly every book in the Old Testament and in his epistles (letters) there are one hundred and ninety-eight quotations from the scriptures.

However wealthy the parents of a Jewish boy, he still had to learn a trade and what better craft than the local one of weaving tent-cloth

A class learning Euclid in a Greek school.

(Acts xviii, 3)? This woven cloth was called "cilicium" after Cilicia; note that the French word for cloak is "cilice".

We know nothing of Saul's mother, but in one of his letters (Rom. xvi, 13) there is a reference to someone "who was also a mother to me" which perhaps indicates that he appreciated a mother's love and care at a time when his own mother had died. His sister was married into a high-priestly family (Acts xxiii, 16) and of high social standing; Saul probably stayed with her whilst training as a student. He must have gone many times to Jerusalem for Passover and other festivals, as one of the many devout pilgrims of the Jewish Dispersion, to worship at the Temple; but we do not know if ever he saw or heard Jesus.

"At the Feet of Gamaliel"

Although Tarsus was a centre of education the University would probably not have admitted him, a Jew, to its learning. In any case, since Saul was being trained for the priesthood, it was necessary for him to complete his education in Jerusalem. He left the synagogue school, therefore, at the age of about seventeen or eighteen, and travelled with great excitement and anxiety to the great city into whose Temple courts he would go, no longer a mere pilgrim but a student. It was his fortune to be under the most famous rabbi in Jerusalem, perhaps in all Palestine, the Pharisee Gamaliel (Acts v, 29). To be accepted by so great a man Saul must have been a most promising pupil—quick, intelligent, eager, "more exceedingly zealous for the Law", determined, with a deep sense of his Jewish faith and its effect upon his life as a "Pharisee of the Pharisees" (Acts xxiii, 6; xxvi, 5). He says of himself, "I advanced beyond many of my age in learning the Jews' religion" (Gal. i, 14; Phil. iii, 6). Gamaliel, as we have seen, was at least tolerant and just, and probably found his young pupil over-impetuous and hasty. Under him Saul learned to argue and discuss and prove his points of the Jewish Law, and eventually qualify as a rabbi to speak with authority in any synagogue in the Roman Empire. Note that he "sat at the feet of Gamaliel"; that was literally true, for students sat on the ground, often on thin mats, to listen to their teachers.

It has been said that Saul was a member of the Sanhedrin, but there is no proof of this. He may have attended some of their meetings as a student in the Law. He may have been present at the trials of Peter and Stephen. If he were absent from Jerusalem at the time Jesus was crucified it is more than likely that what he learned about it was from someone connected with the priests. It is easy to see that this information would have been twisted to make out that Jesus was an impostor and had no right to claim to be the Jews' Messiah. Such wrong ideas about Jesus would make him even more anxious to destroy those connected with Him, for Saul's whole life was now given over to his Jewish religion—the Law and the Tradition.

Saul Begins the Persecutions

From this background you can see that Saul, although Roman by birth, Greek by contact

Saul watched the fisherman mending his nets.

and culture, was trained in the strict faith of the Pharisees; his every move in life was controlled by the Law of Moses and the interpretations put upon that Law by the scribes. It is clear, too, why he would be so furious with Stephen, who, in his own synagogue of the Cilicians, had said that the Law of Moses was no longer powerful and that the crucified Jesus was Messiah. How could the Jews accept a crucified criminal? The Law itself said, "cursed is everyone who is hanged on a tree" (Deut. xxi, 22–23; Gal. iii, 13). Saul himself had probably joined in the arguments but had found Stephen too strong for him, for Stephen was "filled with the Holy Ghost" against Whom no man could stand. Saul's anger at what Stephen had said was fanned by his own feelings of annoyance and inferiority at being worsted in the arguments.

Nablus (Shechem). On Mt. Gerizim, in the background, the Samaritans still celebrate Passover as it was done two thousand years ago.

"Philip's Well", built over the traditional place of the Ethiopian's baptism.

Such beliefs as were held by this Stephen were blasphemous nonsense; he deserved death by stoning (Deut. xiii, 6–10). The whole sect to which he belonged should be killed or cleared out, and he, Saul, "exceeding mad against them", would do it. Only so would the Jewish faith of his fathers be preserved in Jerusalem and Palestine. Thus, he began the first Jewish persecution, and in so doing, deepened and broadened, without knowing it, the rift begun by Stephen. For Saul set out to destroy, not the immediate Jerusalem group of the Apostles still worshipping in the Jewish fashion, but the wider group of Jews and Gentiles beginning to embrace the new beliefs about Jesus—the people of "the Way", the Nazarenes.

With a band of roughs and probably a few armed men, Saul set about his self-appointed task, throwing many of the Nazarenes into prison, possibly killing some, whipping and scourging many. The Hellenists fled to other parts of Judaea, Samaria and beyond. Many of them, of course, returned home (Acts xi, 19, 20). Wherever they went they took with them their Good News (opening the Church to believers in other lands throughout the Roman Empire) even to Antioch, the third city of the empire, and as

far north as Damascus. Saul, in his efforts to destroy the new faith, was spreading it!

Philip the Evangelist

Philip, one of the seven who formed the committee to deal with the administration of the church affairs, was one of those who fled before the fury of Saul. He went to Samaria. In Books II and III we learned how the Samaritans and Jews had hated each other from the time that the Samaritans had offered to help in the rebuilding of the Temple but had been snubbed for their mixed blood by Haggai. Jesus had always made it clear that He thought well of the Samaritans, and now Philip, with the same healing powers of His Master, had come to the capital city to preach about the Man already known by some of the inhabitants. They recalled that this Jesus had met a woman at the well of Sychar and had often passed through the province on His way to Jerusalem; they may have remembered His words about Himself as the promised Messiah (John iv, 25, 26).

In Samaria (Book II) Omri and Ahab had built their magnificent palace. The prophets had foretold the fall of the city in 722 B.C. Years later Herod the Great had rebuilt it in honour of Augustus Caesar, renaming it Sebaste (the Greek name for Augustus). Ruins of the palace, temple and Roman fortifications may still be seen, columns and colonnades reminding us of the grandeur of such cities of long ago. But the Samaritan Jews were ready to listen to Philip. Perhaps they, too, were aware of the uselessness of their ceremonies. They found in Philip's message something more positive and real. Those who believed in Jesus were baptised into the new Church, the first newcomers to what had been until now a purely Jewish community.

The Sorcerer's Magic

Amongst the converts was a sorcerer, a Samaritan, one Simon Magus. He is mentioned in other documents of the time and evidently was well-known for his evil magic arts. Many papyrus fragments and one famous collection of charms, magical formulae, spells and so on, have been found in recent years. These show the kind of gibberish and nonsense chanted by magicians and sorcerers of the day. Simon Magus, Elymas (xiii, 6–11), and the magicians of Ephesus (xix, 13–20) may all have used them in their incantations over the superstitious and frightened people. Here is a cure for people possessed by evil spirits. "Take oil made from unripe olives, with herb mastic and lotus pith, and boil it with marjoram, saying Joel, Ossarthiomi, Emori, Theochipsoith, Sithemeoch, Sothe, Joe, Mimipsothiooph, Phersothi, A.E.I.O.U., come out of him!"

Saul knew the danger of the wolf.

We hear of several occasions when the disciples were hindered by such men whose witchcraft held the superstitious people in great fear. Although he claimed special powers from God, Simon Magus felt that Philip was a greater magician than himself. But as yet there were no signs that the Holy Spirit had come to the new converts; they were not filled with the same ecstasy and understanding of their new faith. This could be given only by Peter and John who now came to see what Philip was doing and to help him. The two apostles saw that deeper prayer and blessing were needed, and when the converts were gathered together in this way the full power of the Holy Spirit came upon them. The change in them was so marked that Simon Magus put it down entirely to the "laying on of hands" which in his sorcerer's mind was a form of magic he would like to possess. It was a perfectly natural idea to him that he could buy this power; Simon Peter made it extremely clear to him that he could not! Legend tells us that Simon Magus became at this time the enemy of Peter, and was so, even in Rome, many years

Not far from Gaza was Ascalon, another Philistine city. These are excavated ruins of a Christian meeting-place in that area.

later. He was there in the reign of Claudius A.D. 41–54. Our word "simony" comes from Simon Magus; it means trying to buy or sell a position or privilege in the Church or getting spiritual power or a favour in church matters by money.

On their way back to Jerusalem Peter and John preached in the Samaritan villages and in this way approved of Philip's "opening of the door" to the Samaritans. Already we see that the faith was being extended beyond Judaea although we should bear in mind that the Samaritans were themselves Jews who also expected their Messiah (Book II, Chapter 10). The faith has not yet accepted the Gentiles.

Philip and the Ethiopian

Meanwhile, Philip had moved southwards along the road to Gaza (see map). The old Philistine city had been razed to the ground in 96 B.C. and was "desert" although the main road to Egypt still ran through it following the "Way of the Philistines" (see Book I, p. 88). The newer city was much nearer the coast. On the way, Philip saw a caravan of pack-animals journeying southwards. In an open chariot sat a dark-skinned man, an African. This was the Treasurer of the Queen Candace of Ethiopia which in those days extended over many lands south of Egypt. Candace was the title of the dynasty or "house", like Pharaoh or Caesar, rather than the personal name of the queen (Book I, p. 28). The Treasurer was a "God-fearer", perhaps a proselyte who had been to Jerusalem for the Feast of Tabernacles. He was reading from the papyrus roll of the Septuagint (LXX), and the passage was the "lesson" for the Feast—Is. liii, 7, 8. This was one of the four poems about the Suffering Servant (Book II, p. 64). He had not understood it whilst at the Feast and was evidently trying to grasp what it meant by reading it out aloud—quite a common habit in the east—as he journeyed. Philip, drawing near, heard him and offered to explain. He told him that the prophecy referred to the crucified and risen Messiah. The Ethiopian believed what Philip told him, and pausing at an oasis to water the animals and rest, suggested that Philip should baptise him. This Philip did and the

Ethiopian went on his way, "rejoicing". We do not know what happened to him when he arrived at his Queen's palace. We can only guess at his conversations. It is possible that he found a Jewish colony and worshipped at their synagogue, and perhaps even there the envious Jews contradicted his belief in a crucified Messiah. Or, perhaps, as Jews of the Dispersion with their freer beliefs, they welcomed him and all he had to tell of his meeting with Philip. Whatever happened, it must have been for much good.

Philip was led on to Azotus (Ashdod), another city of fame under the Philistines (Book I), and thence to Joppa. Here he preached and then went on to Caesarea (Acts xxi, 8, 9) where he had his home. We shall meet Philip again, later in our story.

EXPRESSION WORK

1. Prepare a dialogue between Stephen and Saul.
2. Give Stephen's "Defence" in modern speech.
3. Find suitable headings for each part of Stephen's speech. What entirely new ideas did he put forward?
4. Describe the stoning of Stephen as either Saul or Rhoda (xii, 12–15) might have done to their friends.
5. Learn Phil. iii, 13, 14; iv, 6–8.
6. You visit Tarsus in A.D. 33. Write home a description of what you see.
7. Draw or model a weaver at his loom.
8. "We owe Paul to the prayer of Stephen." What does this mean?
9. Prepare, or give spontaneously, a conversation between Gamaliel and Saul (master and pupil).
10. Why was Saul anti-Christian? How did his efforts to stop the new faith help to spread it further?
11. Imagine that Philip meets the Woman of the Well at Sychar (see Book III, p. 41, and John iv, 5–42). Write down their conversation.
12. Draw Philip talking to the Ethiopian in the chariot,
    or
    Write a Radio Script on the Return of the Ethiopian, showing how he may have brought the "Good News" to the Queen's Court.

CHAPTER 5

THE ROAD TO DAMASCUS

(ix, 1–30)

THE story of the *Acts* now picks up the threads of the persecution begun by Saul, told in viii, 1–3. Thrilled with his first success, Saul offered to go to far-away Damascus in Syria, a journey of 150 miles. He had heard of a strong movement there of the people of "the Way" (viii, 1). The letters obtained from the High Priest could not have been permission to persecute the followers of Jesus, for even the High Priest had no power over foreign synagogues. They were more likely to have been letters of introduction to the rulers of those synagogues and contained recommendations that this young Pharisee should be given all possible help to seek out such people, and then to bring them back to Jerusalem for examination by the Sanhedrin (cf. xxii, 5).

When Luke refers to these members of the new church as "any that were of the Way" (ix, 2) he means "of the Way of Life or Salvation". You will remember that Jesus once said, "I am the Way".

To Damascus

"Breathing threatenings and slaughter" Saul set off along the road through Samaria, on his destroying mission. He was full of excitement and bitter joy. He had tasted success and craved for more; he was zealous for the Jewish faith and would do everything he could to stamp out this new Nazarene religion that was based on the crazy idea that Jesus was the crucified Messiah. His thoughts dwelt upon what he would do in Damascus and how rapidly his fame would spread throughout the land. Damascus he knew as a great caravan city, crowded with travellers and traders. It was there that Eliezer had stayed on his way to Haran to find a wife for Isaac (Book I); Naaman had obeyed Elisha there and had been cured of his leprosy (Book II). The city was surrounded by hills and edged by desert, with miles of gardens intersected with streams and canals alive with pleasure and trading boats. In its booths, bazaars and market squares were silks, gems, ivory, carpets, swords; thirsty travellers quenched their thirst with the juice of lemons cooled with snow from the Hills of Lebanon. Its walls and towers were pierced with massive arches and gates, and through one of these, the Eastern Gate—although he did not dream it—Saul himself was to be led, not as a fearful persecutor but blind, stricken and confused.

His Thoughts

But Saul's mind was not upon Damascus as a city; it was on the arrests he would make and the punishments he would mete to those who were as foolish as Stephen. Stephen—with his talk about Jesus! Jesus? Surely it was in Galilee that He did His preaching? That was where Saul was now riding, along the shore, through Capernaum, across the Hills of Galilee. So this was where the Man had walked and talked. "A Man of sorrows . . . smitten . . . afflicted. . . ." Saul's mind roamed over the scriptures he knew so well. That was how the prophet Isaiah had spoken of the promised Messiah, in his Servant Songs. And Stephen had claimed that this Man Jesus was He Who had been smitten . . . Who had been afflicted . . . Who had suffered . . . Stephen had died in his amazing belief; he had died with great courage, too. Saul had to admit that to himself; it was tremendous courage. He remembered standing by the clothes of those who threw the stones; he saw once more the cut and bleeding face and heard the words of Stephen. It was a prayer he had uttered . . . Saul remembered exactly the words that struggled from the bloodstained lips of the dying man—"Lord, lay not this sin to their charge". An amazing prayer . . . for his enemies . . . Who was this Lord, too?

What Straight Street may have been like.

Was it the Jesus of Whom he had spoken? Could Stephen get so much faith from his belief in Him? Suppose he, Saul, was wrong . . . and that Stephen was right? Even Gamaliel had bidden the Council beware of fighting against God . . . and Stephen had said that Jesus was the Son of God!

We do not really know what thoughts came to Saul as he made his way to Damascus, but in his mind there must have been a turmoil of questions and growing realisation that what he was doing was wrong. It came to him just before Jesus spoke to him in that strange hot lonely place, somewhere on the road, at the parting of the ways. . . . Saul experienced a blinding light, brighter than the sun, that struck him to the ground. He heard a voice that could be no one's but that of Jesus, asking questions that had arisen in his own mind, questions which he knew at last he must answer. "Why are you persecuting Me? Why do you kick like an untamed horse or an obstinate ox against the pricking goad that forces you on? Against the prickings of your own conscience?" Note that Saul answered his own question—"Who art Thou, LORD?" He knew it must be Jesus—Jesus of Nazareth, of Galilee, whose power he had seen in Stephen and in the followers he had already persecuted in Jerusalem. He was later to claim that he had seen Jesus (2 Cor. xii, 1–4; Acts xxiii, 11; 2 Tim, i, 12).

In the City

Blinded by the great light, Saul, a broken figure, was taken to the house of Judas, where for three days and nights he brooded upon his strange experience. Judas lived in Straight Street.

Travellers on the road today.

Women outside modern Nazareth.

The ruins of a synagogue in Jerash (Book III, p. 57) show clearly the Greek influence in its architecture.

We are told that this street ran right through the city and was a mile long. It was a hundred feet wide. Down the centre ran chariots and horsemen and along each side were paths for pedestrians. Ananias (not to be confused with the man of the same name mentioned earlier) was a strict Jew (xii, 12). But like James, the brother of Jesus, in Jerusalem, he was a member of "the Way". Traders in the city market-place had already brought news of Saul's intentions and all believers knew about him by now. It was natural for Ananias to be anxious for he would have been one of the first to be arrested by Saul.

But, told by Jesus that Saul was to be a "chosen vessel" (the Greek really means "vessel of election") or special servant and missionary and His witness to all nations, Ananias did as he was told. Saul received his sight and was baptised into the Church, receiving the power of the Holy Spirit.

It may be useful at this point to read all three accounts of Saul's conversion; each of Saul's

A quiet spell on the Sea of Galilee near Capernaum. The fishermen will soon go out to fish as their ancestors did; they know, too, that a storm may break without warning.

With his goad handy, the ploughman drives his oxen.

Stephen's methods and words. Those who heard him were amazed, but believed he was merely pretending so that he could find out who were the leaders and have them arrested. They decided to get rid of him, to kill him if the need arose. Even the Governor of Damascus, then under the rule of King Aretas IV, "the King who loves his people" as an inscription says, had the gates guarded night and day so that Saul could not escape through them (2 Cor. xi, 32).

In fact, the only way of escape was over the walls. Built along the tops of the walls that circled great cities were houses and watch towers. From one of these houses some of Saul's friends lowered him in a basket. The basket was a tall strong hamper. Saul described it, later, as a net, so it was probably very loosely woven or slung in a net for additional safety (Acts ix, 25; 2 Cor. 32, 33).

own accounts adds to the one given by Luke (ix, 1–18; xxii, 3–16; xxvi, 9–18).

Failure in Damascus

Saul lost no time in going to the synagogue, where he had every right to be, not only as a Jew but also as a rabbi trained under Gamaliel to preach and to explain the Law. But, of course, the Christians were suspicious of him. Was he not there to find out who they were and so trap them? The strict Jews were "confounded" and angry. Saul realised that there was something amiss. He could hardly expect these people to accept him after the rumours they had heard about him. Besides, he himself lacked the deeper experience of his new mission; he needed time to think about his work and to find out what he should do, to prepare a plan of action. You will recall that this was precisely the decision made by Moses, Elijah, John the Baptist and Jesus Himself. So it was that Saul went into Arabia for three years, during which time he could quietly think and pray and plan (Gal. i, 17, 18).

On his return to Damascus, Saul found that many of the Christian Jews were still afraid of him. He preached much on the lines of what Stephen had said, that Jesus was indeed the Messiah. Even after three years he recalled the words of Stephen, so it is not surprising that he copied unconsciously—perhaps deliberately—

Failure in Jerusalem

Saul made for Jerusalem, journeying most of the way on foot and probably recalling his northward trek when he had planned to destroy the very people he now wanted to help. He had failed in Damascus. Now he was entering a veritable lions' den, for he would be meeting the Sanhedrin who had approved of his mission to persecute the Nazarenes.

As we would expect, the Christian Jews in Jerusalem were also suspicious and afraid that he might be spying on them. Three years had passed since he had left the city as Saul the Pharisee; now he had returned as a convert—so he said—to the faith he had gone to destroy. Against him, too, the fury of the High Priests and the Council and the antagonism of his own Hellenist friends from Cilicia and Asia Minor. He was, therefore, welcomed by no one. At last, he found in Barnabas a friend who would listen to him and who believed in his story of what had happened on the Damascus Road. Barnabas told Peter and James and they accepted him also. Saul stayed with Peter for fifteen days. It is a pity that we have no account of what they talked about, but we may be sure that Peter admitted his denials of His Master and told Saul a great deal about His Lord.

But when the Hellenists met Saul they regarded

him as a traitor to their own faith, for they had accepted Judaism to the extent of circumcision. They refused to listen to him as he preached in the very Cilician synagogue where Stephen had taught; they even plotted to kill him. Saul had failed in Jerusalem.

Return to Tarsus

The "brethren" took him to the port of Caesarea and from there he sailed to Tarsus, his home. We may perhaps wonder how Saul and his father met and how he explained to his father the remarkable change in his life. From later references it is believed that Saul then preached for some ten years in Cilicia and Syria (Acts xi, 25; Gal. i, 11–ii, 10) during which time the experiences narrated in 2 Cor. xi, 23–30, may have occurred, since there is no account of them in *Acts*.

Saul's return home was in about A.D. 34. A poem was written, it is said, by a Roman in that same year. It seems to echo some of the thoughts of Saul:

> If Jesus Christ is a Man—
> And only a man—I say
> That of all mankind I cleave to him,
> And to him will I cleave alway.
>
> If Jesus Christ is a god—
> And the only god—I swear
> I will follow Him through heaven and hell,
> The earth, the sea, and the air!

EXPRESSION WORK

1. As Saul, make a verbal request to the High Priest for approval of your decision to go to Damascus to persecute the Nazarenes.
2. As traders in Damascus, tell of Saul's persecutions in Jerusalem. Let Ananias (ix) overhear what is being said, and join in the general discussion of Saul's intentions in Damascus.
3. Pretend you are Saul, riding to Damascus. Speak your thoughts aloud.
4. As one of the Temple Guard riding with Saul, report back to the High Priest with the news of what happened on the road.
5. Dramatise the scene of Saul's attempt to preach in the synagogue of Damascus.
6. Draw a picture of his escape over the walls of Damascus.

Damascus, the oldest inhabited city in the world.

7. Why did Saul fail in (*a*) Damascus, (*b*) Jerusalem?
8. Learn the Roman poem.
9. Prepare a conversation between one of: (*a*) Ananias and Judas, (*b*) Peter and Saul, (*c*) Saul and his father.
10. Write as Barnabas might to his relations in Cyprus, about the new faith and his new friend.
11. How and where do Saul's three accounts of his conversion differ?
12. Prepare for Morning Assembly a Service on the theme of "Called to Serve". Include a reading about a modern missionary.

The old walls of Damascus (Acts ix, 23–25; 2 Cor. xi, 32–33).

CHAPTER 6

ACCEPTING THE GENTILES

(Acts ix, 31–xii, 23)

FROM this time there was peace. We can appreciate the wry smile on Luke's face as he wrote, "Then had the churches rest ..." Saul had given them a great deal of anxiety as a persecutor and not much less as a preacher! Now that he had left them altogether, the churches might settle to quiet progress and organisation.

Peter's Preaching Tour

Peter now moved freely amongst the people, on a preaching tour. He came to Lydda, a village in the fertile plain below the foothills of Judaea. Here he healed Aeneas, a paralysed man. Note that he said, "Jesus Christ healeth thee", not, "I ...". "Make thy bed" means roll it up. It was, of course, a thin mattress or woven mat. This incident is an echo of two miracles performed by Jesus; even Peter's words recall those of Jesus (Mk. ii, 11; John v, 8).

Eight miles away, among its orange groves and on the Mediterranean coast, was Joppa (Jaffa), famed in the days of Solomon when cedars from Lebanon were floated down the coast from Tyre and then sent overland to Jerusalem to be used for the Temple building. Here had lived Dorcas (the Greek name for the Aramaic Tabitha). She had been a loved member of "the Way" and was much mourned when she died. Peter was sent for and when he arrived he found, as had His Master when He had gone to see Jairus' daughter, that the mourners were already there, moaning and wailing as was their custom. Like Jesus, Peter sent them away. Like Jesus, he prayed, and then said "Tabitha, arise". She awoke from her sleep of death. The news spread fast and more believers joined the fast-growing church.

Peter stayed in Joppa, living at the house of another Simon, a tanner of skins. Simon's chief work would be the preparation of whole skins for wine and water. He would see that the ends of the sheep or goatskins once covering the feet and neck were securely closed and then hang each skin in the smoke of a slow-burning fire. In this way the hide was roughly tanned. As the swaying skins hung and twisted over the fire they often appeared like bottles (see Ps. cxix, 83). Pictures of filled skins (Book III) show what these look like; they are still to be seen in Hebron.

Normally, of course, a Jew would not dream of staying with a person of this occupation. For one thing, he was a non-Jew, a Gentile; for another, his work meant handling the skins of dead animals, and this in itself was an "unclean" occupation. But Peter, a Galilean and a disciple of Jesus, was beginning to see that a man's work did not make him any the less acceptable to His Master. He was beginning to change his mind about the people in His Master's Kingdom. He was already seeing that Gentiles themselves might be brought into the Church, and that the keeping of rites and ceremonies of the Jewish Law were not really necessary. As Stephen had said, the Law of Jesus was stronger than the Law of Moses.

Peter and Cornelius

He was to learn this lesson once and for all. Thirty miles along the coast was the Roman garrison city of Caesarea where was stationed a centurion named Cornelius. He was one of the six centurions whose men made up the Italian cohort of 600 soldiers on garrison duty at Headquarters. Like the centurion of Capernaum who had given to the Jews there a very fine synagogue (Book III) Cornelius believed in the Jewish faith and worshipped at the synagogue in Caesarea. But, unlike the other centurion, he did not know Jesus. He was a "God-fearer", one of those who formed the bridge between the two faiths. The Jews probably hoped that he

A stream amid the Judaean hills. Peter probably saw such a peaceful scene as this on his journey.

would eventually accept the full rites of Judaism, be circumcised and be a converted Jew. But, like other proselytes, he was now interested in this new faith by means of which he could become a follower of the Jews' Messiah, and a member of this new church, without first becoming a Jew.

He must have heard about Peter, his preaching and his miracles. Inspired in a vision, he sent to Joppa to ask Peter to come and see him. Two of his reliable slaves and a trusted soldier of his band went on their master's errand.

Meanwhile, possibly thinking over Philip's work in Samaria and his baptising of the Ethiopian, Peter must have pondered on what these events meant for the Kingdom of Jesus. He had gone to the roof-top to meditate. It was the sixth hour of the day—noon—and time for the midday meal. He was hungry and it is not surprising that his thoughts went to food. From the house-top he could see the white sails of ships in the harbour. In his vision, those sails became sheets filled with animals; and a Voice told him to "Kill and eat". Peter saw that the animals were those that a Jew was forbidden to touch; they were "unclean" and "common" (Lev. xi, 1–32, 46, 47). Strict Jews today refuse similar food

for the same reasons; they eat only "kosher" or "clean" meat. When Peter refused to eat, the Voice said, "What God hath cleansed, call thou not unclean." This happened three times.

Still wondering what such a vision could mean, Peter descended the outer stone stairs to the courtyard, where he found three visitors—non-Jews. They had come to see him, on the order of their master, but by the guidance of God. Peter then knew that what he had been told by God was that ceremonial law could be waived, i.e. put on one side or ignored. The Gentiles he had been taught to regard as "unclean" were, in fact, as good as he was. Made, too, by God, they were acceptable to Him. This was a tremendous discovery for Peter to make. Even Caiaphas the High Priest had once refused to go near to a Roman—Pontius Pilate—for fear he would be made "unclean" for the Passover. Now Peter was to go right into the home of a Roman and actually to preach to him. Up till now the Gospel had been only for the Jews; now it was to be given without question to the Gentiles.

At Caesarea

Next day he and some friends started for Caesarea where Cornelius had gathered his

Where the Jerusalem-Lydda-Joppa road enters the Judaean hills.

section of the church for questioning. They charged him with having broken the Jewish law—as he had, of course—by mixing with uncircumcised Gentiles always regarded as "unclean". One of the Jews' ceremonies was to wash up to the elbows before touching food, not because it was hygienic to do so but in order to cleanse themselves from possible contact with Gentiles whilst in the street or market-place or Temple Court.

Peter did not "explain"; he merely recounted his vision and what followed it, pointing out that the Romans had received the Lord's unmistakable baptism of the Holy Spirit—and who was he "to withstand God"? The Jews accepted this as the sign that God had opened the Church to the Gentiles also, but, as we shall see, many of them had misgivings and were not fully satisfied. In any case, these occasions were reasonably near to Jerusalem and there was no sign, as yet, that it would spread.

Antioch in Syria

Meanwhile, persecuted Jews of the Dispersion had done great work in cities throughout

household and friends. The day after, the apostle arrived. Cornelius greeted him as one sent from God and in kneeling gave Peter the homage he would have given to any of his Roman gods. Peter bade him remember that he was but a man, adding that as a Jew he really ought not to enter the house. He looked around the room with its marble and mosaic floor, furnished with Roman tables and divans, hung with silk curtains. He saw men and women in their Roman togas and gowns, soldiers resplendent in their various ranks and uniforms, slaves peeping from doorways. Peter was far from overawed. Nor did he feel "unclean" in this Gentile house. There was something in the atmosphere that made him feel the presence of God and His Master. He asked, "Why have you sent for me?" Cornelius told him of his vision and Peter knew that he was to break down the last barrier of the new faith and accept these Gentiles into "the Way".

So he preached to them the Risen Christ, and as he did so the power of the Holy Spirit came upon them all. Thrilled with their new experience, they "spoke with tongues" and burst into praise. Even Peter and his friends were amazed at what could be but a miracle—that Gentiles should receive the Holy Spirit. Peter, now convinced and, as always, a man of action, ordered baptism with water as the formal sign that the Roman household had been admitted into the church.

Peter in Jerusalem

We are not surprised to find that on his return to Jerusalem Peter was sent for by the Jewish

An aerial view of the modern Jerusalem-Jaffa (Joppa) road.

The view of modern Jaffa from the house of Simon the Tanner.

Phoenicia, Cyprus and Syria, whose capital city Antioch—known for its idolatry and superstitious beliefs—became, amazingly, the new centre of the Christian faith in that district. The city— "Queen of the East", "Antioch the Beautiful", the third city of the Roman Empire—was a Greek city named after Antiochus I in 300 B.C. (Book II, Chapter 11). It was now much larger, having been captured in 64 B.C. and developed by the Romans. Many of its people were pleasure-loving with little thought for anything but wealth, luxury and selfish enjoyment: some, as we shall see, had higher thoughts of life and worship.

Antioch was sixteen miles up-river from the Great Sea, standing on the bank of the River Orontes, with Seleucia as its seaport. A huge statue of Charon, the ferryman of the dead across the River Styx in Hades, had been cut out of the mountainside on the orders of the hated Antiochus Epiphanes. It overlooked the colonnaded white marble avenue that ran straight and Roman-true for nearly five miles from east to west of the city. The city walls must have been tremendous, for remains today show parts eleven feet wide and forty feet high with look-out towers every fifty yards. The ruins of Trajan's aqueduct, a huge amphitheatre for gladiatorial displays and chariot racing, remind us of the

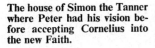

The house of Simon the Tanner where Peter had his vision before accepting Cornelius into the new Faith.

Peter saw his vision on the flat roof-top.

there. Traders from faraway lands with their enormous caravans moved to and from its markets, thronging the bazaars and booths, bartering with metalworkers, leatherworkers, dyers, dealing in silks, cloths, spices and pottery. Yet, to its busy streets had come a group of Nazarenes, some from Cyprus—the island off the coast—many from Jerusalem. By their preaching these had brought the Good News of the Kingdom of Jesus. And people had listened and believed. They had thrown away their gods and charms, and had accepted the happiness and joy offered by the new teaching.

"Called Christians in Antioch"

Someone in Antioch must have referred to

The triclinium in Cornelius' house (see Book III, p. 49).

Roman feats of building and engineering. All the luxury of Rome and the magnificence of Greece was in Antioch—public baths, central heating, street lighting, drainage systems, fountains, arenas, temples, gardens and statues. The well-to-do lived in well-designed villas; the less wealthy occupied blocks of several storeys like our modern blocks of flats.

The whole world seemed to meet in the streets of Antioch—Syrians, Jews, Greeks, Romans, Phoenicians, Phrygians, Egyptians. The Imperial Legate or Caesar's Chief Governor was stationed

their belief in Christ—perhaps in scorn and contempt, perhaps only in jest—for he called them "Christ-ians"—Christians. It was only a nickname, but from that time it was a name borne by all followers of Jesus; to this day we are called by the same name (Acts xxvi, 28; 1 Peter iv, 16).

This sudden extension of the Church annoyed the Jews in Jerusalem. They still did not accept the claim that the crucified Jesus was the Christ, the promised Messiah; they preferred to call these people the Nazarenes. But the name "Christian" had come to stay.

It was not long before the apostles in Jerusalem became anxious about this branch of the Nazarene church for a very different reason. Here was

Cornelius may have had a villa like this.

a serious challenge to the main sect in Jerusalem, for it was seen that races other than Jews were joining the Christians and the longed-for dream that Israel had of being God's chosen nation seemed to be shattered. These Gentiles were un-circumcised and therefore "unclean"; surely it was necessary for them to be "made obedient unto the law"—to be made full Jews—before being accepted. If not, they could even pass beyond the barrier in the Temple Court, and this would break for ever the covenant between Moses and God (Acts xxi, 27–30).

Of course, Peter had accepted Cornelius and the heads of the Church in Jerusalem had seen the reason and felt that this was an isolated occasion. But this movement in Antioch was much more serious. They must find out more about it. They did not go themselves, but sent someone on their behalf. This was Barnabas, friend of Saul, "a good man and full of the Holy Ghost". He was a Cypriot, too, and would therefore be able to speak more easily with people of his own land who had begun the move-ment by their preaching in Syria. Barnabas went to the meeting-place of the Christians in Antioch; tradition says it was in Singon Street. After a while he may have felt it was necessary to have someone with greater powers of speech and leadership than he possessed, someone who had a wide and deep knowledge of the scriptures, too, a Jew who believed in Jesus as His Risen Lord, someone who knew the city and its people. There was only one such man—Saul of Tarsus.

So Barnabas went to Tarsus and found Saul; this was in about A.D. 45. Over ten years had passed since Saul had gone home and he was now ready for whatever work he was given to do. He was His Master's "chosen vessel" to bear the Good News throughout the world. Together, they returned to Antioch and joined the Christians, preaching and working there for a year.

Famine in Judaea

At this time a Christian prophet, Agabus, foretold a famine for Jerusalem and Judaea. History tells us that there was in fact a famine during the early years of Claudius, one of the Roman Emperors of this period (A.D. 41–54).

An ancient gateway to a synagogue.

Gifts of money and food were made by the Church in Antioch and these were given to Barnabas and Saul and Titus to take to the Apostles in Jerusalem. We can imagine the great joy of the Christians there at seeing the donkeys and camels laden with sacks and bags of corn, raisins, figs, and the skins of olive oil and wine (Gal. ii, 1). It was possible that Barnabas and Saul told the leaders of the Jerusalem Church that they planned to visit the cities of Asia Minor in a preaching tour (Gal. ii, 1–10; Acts xi, 30). On their return to Antioch they took with them John Mark (Col. iv, 10), related to Barnabas; he was but a youth, but anxious to be with two great men on a mission that promised excitement and adventure. You will

Coins of Emperor Claudius, A.D. 41–54

This arch is at Antioch in Pisidia.

remember that his mother's house was the meeting-place of the Apostles and where Jesus had held His Last Supper. John Mark knew Jesus well; he had even seen Him arrested (Mark xiv, 51, 52). He looked forward to telling other people about His Master.

Persecution in Jerusalem

Since the stoning of Stephen and the consequent fleeing of persecuted Hellenist Jews, things had been reasonably peaceful and quiet. The Apostles, trying desperately to fit their new teaching about Jesus into the framework of their own Jewish religion, had been left alone. They had continued within Judaism their own meetings and services and forms of worship.

In A.D. 39, in place of Herod Antipas—murderer of John the Baptist—had come Herod Agrippa I, grandson of Herod the Great, nephew of Herod Antipas (Books II and III). Agrippa had been given Perea and Galilee, the tetrarchies of Philip and Antipas, by the Emperor Caligula who had favoured him in Rome. Claudius then gave him Judaea and Samaria, together with the title of King. As a Jew he opposed the idea that the crucified Christ could possibly be the Messiah; as a favourite of the Emperor he could not

tolerate any suggestion of another king. He therefore decided to crush out any believers still left in the land. He knew he would have on his side at least the Pharisees and Sadducees.

He chose Passover as his best time to strike. Just before the feast he sent his soldiers to arrest James, the brother of John, the "beloved disciple". You will recall that James and John, the sons of Zebedee, together with Peter, were the three disciples closest to Jesus. Because it was so near Passover, James' trial—if he had one—was short and, like that of His Master, entirely unlawful. James was executed with the sword, the first apostle to die for Jesus.

Agrippa's next arrest was swift. Peter was thrown into prison, below the dungeon of Antonia. When Passover was ended he would have Peter killed also. Perhaps Agrippa had heard of Peter's previous escape, so he had him securely chained between two soldiers, with two more on duty outside the cell. Each four were a "quaternion".

Peter's Escape

In some miraculous way—a story vividly told by Luke in xii, 3–19—Peter was once again freed. Luke seems to intend the story to be taken as it stands, but some people prefer to think it is a description of Peter's release by some mysterious friend, arguing that the word "angel" means "messenger" and could be a man. Even so, Peter's rescue was remarkable. He hastened to the Upper Room where he knew his friends would be gathered in prayer and anxiety for his safety. Rhoda's first peep through the grating in the door was in fear and trembling lest the knock was that of a searching soldier with a guard to arrest the other Apostles. In her excited joy she returned to tell the others without letting Peter in! "It is his angel," they said. Already there was a belief in a kind of guardian angel (Matt. xviii, 10). We remember that the influence of such a belief came from Persia (Books II and III). (See also in the Apocrypha, Tobit v, 21, where the angel actually travels with Tobias.) At first unbelieving, then silently, they admitted Peter who told them how he had escaped.

He bade them tell the other James, the brother of Jesus, now chief or president of the church in Jerusalem. Next morning, the Roman guard had an amazing escape to "explain", but Agrippa did not believe them and had them executed, the penalty for failing in their duty.

Death of Agrippa

Agrippa then went to Caesarea, where a quarrel with Tyre and Sidon was settled. He had a hold over these two towns because they obtained their corn from his province of Galilee and could not afford to be his enemies. The king held, in great majesty and extravagance, special shows of pomp and power. There were displays in the huge amphitheatre—gladiators, athletes, conjurors, chariot-racing and the like. He dressed himself in beautiful robes and jewels and the people called out that he was a god. Thousands took up the cry and Herod Agrippa accepted their flattery and fawning praise. A writer of the times, Josephus, says that Agrippa saw an owl on a rope over his head—an evil omen. Luke tells us simply that the king was struck with dreadful pains and was dead in three days. The people saw in it a deserved punishment for his wickedness in claiming to be a god. What is of real importance is that the first great enemy of the Christian Church had gone. Had he lived to pursue his persecution of the church in Jerusalem, the story of Christianity might perhaps not have been written. This was in A.D. 44, after which the lands under Agrippa were put under the complete control of Rome. History tells us that there were outbreaks of rioting, rebellion and revolts. We already know

that the famine in Judaea had been foretold and this happened in about A.D. 46, leading to further suffering and bloodshed.

EXPRESSION WORK

1. Read the accounts of Jesus healing the paralysed man and Jairus' daughter. In what ways did Peter's miracles resemble these?
2. Draw Simon tanning his skins.
3. Prepare a radio or TV script of the story of Peter and Cornelius,
   or
   Show the story in strip cartoon.
4. Imagine that the Centurion of Capernaum meets Cornelius. What do they talk about?
5. Model or sketch a Roman villa such as Cornelius might have had. Pictures in history books will help you.
6. What lesson did Peter learn? Was it important? Why? Explain: "Peter unlocked the door to the Gentiles; Paul pushed it wide open."
7. What did Peter mean by Acts xi, 17?
9. Why was it (a) strange, (b) not surprising, that Antioch in Syria should become the centre of Christianity?
10. Why were the Jerusalem Jews perturbed at what was happening in Antioch and elsewhere? Why did they send Barnabas to Antioch?
11. Act in mime "Peter's Escape", *or* as Rhoda, tell what happened to friends on the next housetop.
12. Why was Herod Agrippa II the first great enemy of the Christian Church?

Routes from all parts of the Roman Empire converged upon Antioch, a stronghold that became the centre of Christianity.

CHAPTER 7

THE FIRST MISSIONARY JOURNEY

(xiii, xiv)

Chosen for the Work

SINCE there were no Apostles in Antioch, the church there was organised under a small committee of five members. It is interesting to note that three of them were white, two black; and one of them at least was a wealthy man, the half-brother of Herod the tetrarch. They discussed the work to be done and decided that the Good News should be sent further afield. Who should take it? God's guidance (the Holy Spirit) was asked. Barnabas and Saul were chosen. This was somewhat strange, for neither of them was an original member of the group in Antioch. They had come, one as a delegate and the other as a preacher. But the Christians accepted the decision not only because the choice had fallen to them and was believed to be God's will, but also because they recognised in Barnabas and Saul the two men who could best do the work.

Ignatius

It may well have been that at this very meeting in Singon Street was a lad of fifteen. Thirty years later he became the first Bishop of Antioch, Bishop Ignatius. An old man of 75, Ignatius was martyred for his faith. Sent to Rome in A.D. 108, on the orders of Trajan, he was flung to the lions in the amphitheatre. His last words were, "Let me be given to the wild beasts for through them I can attain unto God. I am God's wheat and I am ground by the wild beasts that I may be found pure bread of Christ."

Barnabas and Saul

Perhaps we wonder what these two men were like. It is difficult to say, of course, with any certainty, but some indication of their appearance may be gleaned from the narratives and letters of Paul.

Barnabas, trained as a Levite and a strict Jew, seems to have been the elder of the two, well-built and good-looking, with honest eyes and a firm mouth and chin. In Lystra the people called him Jupiter, one of the noblest of the Roman gods, and this makes it certain that he was of fine physique. We know from the fact that he was one of the first to sell his lands and give the money to the poorer members of the early church that his religion really meant something to him. He was mild and generous, sympathetic and approachable, the "Son of Consolation". That he was a shrewd judge of character is evident, for he recognised in Saul a promising preacher and servant of God. Barnabas brought Saul from obscurity to Christian service such as the world has never since seen (Acts ix, 27; xi, 25, 26).

Saul—later called *Paul*—was now about forty-five years of age. He seemed to differ considerably from Barnabas in build and appearance. A second century document describes him in most uncompromising terms as "a man small in size, with meeting eye-brows, with a rather large nose, baldheaded, bow-legged. Strongly built, full of grace, for at times he looked like a man, and at times he had the face of an angel." Whatever his body, often racked with pain and fever, his face and voice had strange powers of attraction. At Lystra the people hailed him as Mercury, the messenger of the gods, small, swift, eloquent of speech; his physical courage is indicated in 2 Cor. xi, 24. Some people believe that his eyesight was probably affected by the blinding light of his conversion (Gal. vi, 6) or by painful headaches. He may have had a tendency to attacks of malaria or some other physical disability. Whatever this "stake (thorn) in the flesh" (2 Cor. xii, 7–10) was, it was a great trial to him; you will be able to assess his courage, judgment and devotion to his duty as you study his missionary work and read his letters.

Paul's Methods

Not the least of the indications of Paul's clear mind is the way he set about his task. There was

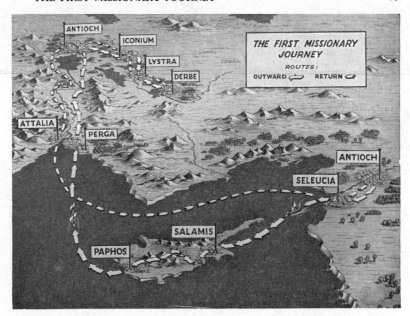

Follow on this map the journey of Paul. Remember the difficulties of travel in those days—rocky roads, robbers, wild animals.

never anything haphazard about his methods. As we study the journeys we recognise his amazing ability to organise. A first glance at his travels may give the impression that his work was casual, but in actual fact he was systematic. Province by province, he moved into the chief cities for his main centres; he set up Christian groups—churches—and appointed elders whose work it was to unite the community into a kind of "mother church". When this was secure it spread its activities into the surrounding districts and smaller towns. A good example of this is seen in the church at Ephesus with its smaller church at Colossae. Paul then revisited these churches, or sent trained helpers, or wrote to explain, encourage, guide, reprove and praise.

We shall find that Paul was a wise and deep thinker. Like Jesus he spent much time in prayer and quiet meditation. His language was practical. In Athens he spoke as a philosopher to philosophers, in Lystra in simple Greek about their Creator, in Pisidian Antioch as a Jew to the Jews. Once he had won his argument at the Council of Jerusalem he set out to create a World Church (Gal. iii, 28), and was able to adapt his words to the various peoples of that church.

Learning the journeys of Paul as a string of "places visited and what happened" is not the

The harbour scene at Seleucia as Paul, Barnabas and John Mark leave for Cyprus.

Here, the ship is off the coast and making for Cyprus.

best way to get to know Paul. Try to think of him as a man of tireless energy, a hero, a lover of adventure, and afraid of no one. He was one who attracted men and women to his cause and inspired them to work for and with him. He was a missionary and a saint; no one did more to help in the growth and development of the Christian church. All the incidents of which we shall read illustrate various aspects of a very wonderful man who explained his secret in his letter to the Philippians—"I can do all things through Christ who strengtheneth me."

The Journey Begins

In about A.D. 47, then, we find Barnabas and Saul and John Mark setting off on their first new adventure. The most obvious direction was towards Cyprus, partly because it was the nearest "new land" and also because it was the homeland of Barnabas who wanted to preach first to his own people. The name Cyprus comes from a word meaning "copper"; there were copper mines in the interior of the island.

The three men sailed the sixteen miles down the River Orontes to the port of *Seleucia* where they boarded a small boat (large ones could not get into the harbour) to cross the eastern part of the Great Sea to the island (see map). They landed at *Salamis*, the commercial centre of the island. Here there was trading in copper, olive

oil, wine and fruits. There was a great temple to Zeus and in the city were three forums or market-places, public baths and huge colonnaded buildings. Granite columns, called "St. Paul's Pillars", and remains of a temple still stand as they did in these times, but sand covers the rest which years later were levelled to the ground in severe earthquakes. Legend says that Barnabas was stoned to death in Salamis; his body was recovered by Mark and buried outside the city.

As was his custom—for Saul always preached first to his own people, the Jews—he went to the synagogue and explained his mission, preaching that the crucified Jesus was the Messiah of the new faith. Barnabas probably took the lead here, and John Mark assisted as a young helper.

They travelled through the island to the western tip where stood *PAPHOS*. This was the capital city and the residence of the Roman pro-consul Sergius Paulus. Valuable inscriptions have been unearthed at Paphos, giving much interesting detail about the family of the governor. Amongst other information we learn that his wife and one of his sons became Christians and that another son followed his father as a Roman official in the island.

Elymas

Elymas (Bar-Jesus=Son of Salvation) was a sorcerer or magician—like Simon Magus—with some considerable power and position. It was natural that he should regard Saul with some jealousy, and as a rival. He saw that his own position was precarious if the pro-consul accepted what Saul had to say. Saul, being a Roman citizen, well-educated and cultured, was the equal socially of Sergius Paulus, and they enjoyed each other's company. Like most Romans, the governor was interested in this new religion. Barnabas, too, was probably well-known as a land-owner in the island. So Elymas began to feel a little disturbed. His own power seems to have been that of hypnotism. Luke, a doctor, makes it clear that Saul treated him, as we say, with "his own medicine". He "fixed his eyes upon him". Elymas could not withstand the strength of Saul's eyes; his blindness and consequent defeat ruined him in the eyes of the islanders. From this time, Paul uses his Roman name and becomes the chief speaker, and Barnabas tends to drop into the background. Even Luke reverses the order in which he speaks of them, and says . . . "Paul and Barnabas. . . .". The events described brought many to accept the Christian faith, for they and Sergius Paulus were "astounded at what Paul taught about the Lord Jesus".

John Mark Returns

There was probably a trading ship bearing copper, fruits (lemons and olives), olive oil and wine, on its way from Paphos to the coast of Asia Minor. The friends boarded the ship which sailed due north, putting in at *Perga*, about eight miles up river. Paul may have suffered from the effects of malaria whilst staying here, in this low-lying area of marshland and swamps, so he decided to press forward into the higher healthier mountain range that loomed in the distance. But he was to be much disappointed before he did so, for John Mark now made up his mind to return home. We do not know why, but there may have been many reasons. He was but a lad and was probably homesick; perhaps he was afraid of the perils of the mountain journey. The nearest town of any size was a hundred miles away, through dangerous mountain paths and by lonely roads. In the pine woods that fringed the foothills lurked bandit murderers and wild beasts; the

A marble forum, excavated at Salamis.

thought of what these might do must have made him fearful.

Perhaps, too, John Mark was a little jealous of Paul's success. He was disappointed at seeing his cousin Barnabas take second place; it meant that he, John, was a little less important, too. Barnabas did not blame Mark and was perhaps more sympathetic towards him than was Paul; but that Paul was really angry at what he regarded as weakness and cowardice is seen later, when he planned the second journey and refused to take Mark with him (Acts xv, 36–40; but see also 2 Tim. iv, 11). Mark joined another ship bound for Caesarea or Joppa and so returned to Jerusalem.

The Roman bath is surrounded by marble statues.

In Paphos—a Greek church on the site of a Roman temple. Legend says that Paul was tied to one of these pillars and beaten.

To Antioch in Pisidia

Meanwhile, Paul and Barnabas and his friends—"the company"—continued their dangerous way over the forbidding Taurus Mountains, "in perils often" from man and beast, until they at last reached the city of *ANTIOCH*. This city was called Pisidian Antioch to distinguish it from two other Antiochs, one of these being Paul's starting point in Syria. Actually, it was in Phrygia, but lay very near the border of the neighbouring province of Pisidia.

The Taurus Mts. probably over-awed Mark (Acts xiii, 13).

Once a Greek city, it was now a Roman colony, fortified and garrisoned, of course, with Roman legionaries to assist the ex-service men already settled there as part of the Roman plan for law and order. It was the chief city of the Roman province of Galatia, which included the smaller lands already mentioned. A fine Roman aqueduct brought water from the hills; now the city is gone and the aqueduct a mass of rubble and stones.

It was a prosperous city, and, as was usual in the larger towns, there was a Jewish quarter of the many Jews who had come to Antioch to trade and make money. They had their own synagogue, of course. The Romans worshipped their own goddess Cybele—sometimes called Diana or Artemis, the Great Mother of All—in a magnificent temple.

As usual, when Paul was sufficiently recovered from his illness and the tiring journey, they entered the synagogue. We remember that synagogue services were exactly the same throughout the Jewish settlements, and wherever a Jew went he could follow and understand them. Among the congregation were the usual proselytes, the "God-fearers". Paul and Barnabas probably took with them on their journeys their precious fringed "taliths" or praying tunics. (Nowadays in Jewish synagogues men wear praying-shawls as taliths.) The ruler or chief rabbi, called the *chazzan*, noticing the two strangers of authority, invited them to speak.

Paul and Barnabas knew their Jewish Law thoroughly and Paul, at least, was a fully qualified rabbi. He took the lead, as we might expect.

Paul's Speech

We have here the first recorded speech of Paul. It is significant in its form, for it follows very nearly the speeches of both Peter and Stephen. In places it is strongly reminiscent of Stephen and we cannot help but think that Paul had him in mind as he spoke. He preached to the Jews first, to the proselytes afterwards—to the "men of Israel and you who heed God". He traced the history of the Jews and won his hearers by the sheer power of his words and obvious knowledge, his quotations from the scriptures strengthening each point made. He told them that the Messiah had come (23, 24). He had been crucified—that must have horrified them. God had raised Him from the dead. . . . What were they to make of that? This, said Paul, was proof of the Messiahship of Jesus and that obedience to Him was of greater importance than obedience to the Law. This was indeed a new teaching for these Jews. By keeping the Law they were endeavouring to "keep on the right side" of God. They found it hard to do this and therefore felt that they could never obtain the full goodness of God. But Paul said that Christianity made it possible for them to come to God in their weakness and He would make them strong. It was Christ who had

A modern road winds through the precipitous Cilician Gates.

brought forgiveness for the sins they committed in not reaching the standard of living set by their own Law, and people had only to believe in Christ to be "saved". The Christian did not serve God to keep on the right side of Him, but because he was glad Jesus had lived, died and risen again for him. The Jews were interested and the proselytes were most impressed. Here was a

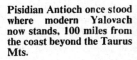

Pisidian Antioch once stood where modern Yalovach now stands, 100 miles from the coast beyond the Taurus Mts.

Transport today where Paul once travelled in Asia Minor. He probably joined a caravan for company and safe journeying.

religion they could follow without accepting those tiresome rites and ceremonies of the Jews. What was more important, it was a religion they could understand and believe in. We need to remember that at such a distance from Jerusalem these Jews—Hellenist Jews of the Dispersion—were out of touch with the real facts of the Crucifixion and certainly of the Resurrection, although some of them had been there for the festivals. So Paul's preaching was astonishing in every way and they needed time to think about what he had said. They asked him to speak to them on the following sabbath.

"Lo, We turn to the Gentiles"

During the week, however, some of the stricter Jews realised that Paul was offering his message to the Gentiles as well. They were jealous, for the Messiah was theirs alone. His chosen people were the Jews and only the Jews. So we are not surprised to find that immediately Paul began his sermon on the following sabbath, the Jews interrupted him and tried to stop him. Paul was at first perplexed, then hurt, then furious. His next words were not a hasty decision. For many years he must have given careful thought to what he was now about to say; and he must have talked it over with Barnabas. Though himself a strict Jew he had known all along that Jesus had died for *all* His people. On the guidance of the Apostles in Jerusalem he had come to preach to the Jews only, though the Gentiles might also listen and believe, too. But now, the Jews were the very ones who were preventing him from spreading his Good News. They were denying him and defying him—even blaspheming the holy name of Jesus. Let it be so, said Paul. Seeing that they were unworthy of everlasting life—"lo, we turn to the Gentiles!"

The Jews could hardly believe their ears, but the Gentiles heard him with great joy. This tremendous decision was the turning point of the Christian Church, a complete revolution. For it meant that now all Gentiles who believed in the risen Christ could accept Him and be accepted by the Church without the rules, regulations and ceremonies of the Jews. This was a religion of Love—Love for and obedience to a *Person*, and this could replace obedience to laws and rules.

A month or so passed, but the Jews had been plotting. Urged on by the influential "honourable women" of the synagogue—the wives and daughters of wealthy Roman proselytes—the angry Jews planned to drive Paul and Barnabas from the city. In the interests of law and order, the city magistrates instructed the two to leave.

They did so. On the outskirts of the city they took off their sandals and shook them to show that they regarded the Jews as having hindered their work (see Matt. x, 14 and Luke ix, 5).

Towards the East

The missionaries made their way along the fine new road for some ninety miles, when they came to *Iconium* (Konieh), a Greek city of Phrygia on the borders of Lycaonia. It was high on the plateau of Asia Minor, the mountains rearing to the north-west (see map). This journey was considerably less difficult because there was easier means of transport, perhaps by mule, even in a wagon of some kind. There were marching soldiers on the route, travellers, traders, long strings of camels laden with merchandise, pilgrims and, occasionally, Roman processions of wealthy people returning to or from the far coast (Gal. iv, 15). Wayside khans and inns offered rest and food and conversation by the brazier, and Paul and Barnabas would learn much from traders and pilgrims; they in turn would speak of Jesus and so spread their work farther afield than they would ever know.

Acts xiv, 1, tells us that many of the Jews accepted what Paul had to say, but the rulers of the synagogues were jealous of the Greeks who showed great interest. Arguments led to violence and the two decided it would be safer to leave the town and proceed to *LYSTRA*.

In Lystra

This city, some twenty miles further south-west, was mainly a Roman colony, with its Jewish and Greek quarters. Here they were welcomed and stayed four or five months. During this time it is more than likely that Paul saw the altar dedicated to Augustus Caesar as a god and realised more vividly that here was something he would have to contend with in the future—the worship of the Roman Emperor. For to preach against such a thing would be treason—and that would mean death. This altar still stands on the hill outside Lystra—or Lustra, as the Romans called it.

Paul's first recorded miracle was performed here. The healing of the lame man was done "in the name of Jesus". There was a legend in Lystra that the gods Zeus (Roman Jupiter) chief of the gods, and Hermes (Roman Mercury) messenger of the gods, had once appeared and had been rejected by all the people except Philemon and Baucis who had been the only survivors of the flood sent by the gods as punishment. Now, seeing the miracle, the people immediately imagined that the gods had come again. They shouted and argued excitedly in their Lycaonian tongue which was unfamiliar to Paul who did not at first realise what they were about to do. But when he saw them preparing a sacrifice at the gates of the temple of Jupiter outside the city, he knew at once. He and Barnabas had to rush from the market-place to stop the priests, tearing their cloaks as they did so as a sign of grief and distress.

Paul spoke to them in Greek, a tongue they would all understand. He spoke of God as the Creator of all Nature and urged them to change their ways. The mob were gradually restrained from their first intentions and slowly realised that the two were merely men. In this mood of disappointment they were easily encouraged into anger, and it needed very little cunning on the part of jealous Jews, who had by now come from Iconium and Antioch, to stir them against Paul and Barnabas. It needed only one stone to begin their attack and, like the first martyr Stephen whose death he had watched, Paul was struck to the ground. Bruised and bleeding from sharp-edged rocks, his maimed body was left for dead and for the vultures to swoop upon and devour. But, unlike Stephen, Paul recovered; he had great work for His Master yet to do.

In the fiendish crowd, jostled and frightened

A Roman chariot.

The ruined Temple of Jupiter in Baalbek, 35 miles from Damascus. Perhaps the temple at Lystra was similar to this one.

and anxious for Paul, was a young lad named Timothy (xvi, 1) who was to remember this dreadful incident for many years (2 Tim. iii, 11, 14, 15). It may have been his mother Eunice and his grandmother Lois who attended to Paul and nursed him in secret. We shall hear of Timothy again.

The Return to Antioch

They made a short visit to *Derbe*, where Gaius was converted. Near Derbe—even to this day—are found Roman milestones marking the route at every one thousand paces, and Greek altars amongst fragments of pottery, granite and marble. Paul and Barnabas decided not to go farther eastwards. Perhaps Paul wanted to do his work in Roman territory. The Jews had not come to Derbe, probably because they believed that Paul was now dead. But the two friends returned fearlessly through *Lystra* and *Iconium*. It seems that they were allowed there because they did not speak openly. Their work was to organise the groups of believers into churches whose "elders" could then control the work to be done. They continued to Pisidian *Antioch*.

We now find that Luke's narrative moves swiftly and with very little detail. The "apostles", as the two are now called, preach in Pisidia and Pamphylia and then set sail from *Attalia*, south-eastwards to *Seleucia* and thence to *Antioch* in

Syria—home, after an absence of two years and a journey of fourteen hundred miles!

Jews and Gentiles

Paul and Barnabas went at once to Singon Street where they recounted their adventures and success. The Christian church listened with joy to all they had to say, but were especially impressed when Paul told them how God had "opened the door of faith unto the Gentiles". This door of faith was the acceptance of Gentiles into the church without their having to take upon themselves the full burden of the Jewish Law and Tradition. It was, of course, not the Jewish faith but the new Christian faith based on belief in Jesus the crucified as the risen Messiah. This was certain to be questioned by the Christian Jews in Jerusalem. These insisted that all Gentiles wishing to enter the church must first be circumcised according to the Law of Moses and become Jews. Circumcision was the outward sign of the Covenant between God and His chosen people. All Jewish baby boys were circumcised when only eight days old by a simple operation on the sex organ; it was a definite Law of Moses (Gen. xvii, 10–13; Lev. xii. 3; Luke ii, 21). The Jews therefore argued that if the Gentiles were also to be accepted as chosen people, it was only right that they should first become Jews by circumcision. Delegates were sent from Jerusalem to

Antioch to make this plain to the church there. Amongst them may have been Peter, for Paul tells us in Gal. ii, 11–14, that he argued with Peter over this question, pointing out that Peter himself had accepted Gentiles (Cornelius, especially) and had eaten with them. But Peter had shown some fear of what the other Jews of Jerusalem thought, until Paul chided him for trying to make the Gentiles do what he was not doing himself. Perhaps this is why we find Peter on the side of Paul at the meeting in Jerusalem, when the whole subject was discussed.

Epistle to Galatians

It was necessary for Paul and Barnabas to report to Jerusalem on their tour; in any case, Paul was determined to settle once and for all the position of the Gentiles. It is accepted by many scholars that it was on his way to Jerusalem that Paul wrote his letter to the churches he had visited in Galatia. This would now be in about A.D. 48–49 (Acts xi, 1–18; xv, 1–29; Gal. i, 15–ii, 14). Other scholars prefer to date it somewhat later, A.D. 52. It was written to the pagan people who had become members of the churches Paul and Barnabas had set up. It is an angry letter. Some Jewish Christians from Jerusalem had sent preachers to these churches to say that Paul's teaching was false and that the people should accept circumcision like the Apostles in Jerusalem and become full Jews. Paul was furious, yet astonished that such lies should not only be spoken but actually believed. To him the survival of the Christian church was at stake (Gal. vi, 15). He is angry and tender by turns; sometimes he is bitter and affectionate. He emphasises his own authorship by signing his name. He does this in large letters, perhaps due to his bad eyesight. Read his letter in a modern version.

EXPRESSION WORK

1. Prepare a conversation between Saul, Barnabas and John Mark, discussing plans for their first journey.
2. Relate the events of Paphos as one of: Elymas, John Mark, Sergius Paulus, a slave in the household.
3. Let John Mark explain to Barnabas why he wants to go back to Jerusalem, *or*

Interview him for an article in the "Jerusalem Times".
4. Find all you can about Ignatius of Antioch. Give a talk about him to the class.
5. How did Paul's speech (*a*) resemble, (*b*) differ from, that of Stephen?
6. "Lo, we turn to the Gentiles." What was the significance of this decision?
7. Draw Paul and Barnabas on their way to Iconium.
8. Dramatise the events at Lystra.
9. Prepare for Morning Assembly a Service on the theme of "Brotherhood".
10. Learn Gal. v, 22–23, 25; vi, 7.
11. Explain Gal. iii, 28.
12. Prepare a frieze to illustrate the First Missionary Journey, *or*
Model in clay, household cement, etc., a map of the Mediterranean; show the places visited and label the chief events.

Jupiter, the chief Roman God.

CHAPTER 8

THE COUNCIL AT JERUSALEM

(xv)

The Dispute

IT is clear that Paul does not agree with the demands of the Apostles in Jerusalem and that a meeting between them is likely to be one of arguments and bitterness unless they can come to a solution to which they can all agree. We do not know where they met, but it is possible that they gathered at the house of John Mark, in the familiar Upper Room.

James, the brother of Jesus, was now Bishop of Jerusalem. The word "Bishop" here does not mean quite the same as it does today; James was the president or chief apostle of the Christian Church of the believing Jews. He was, of course, a strict Jew and kept the usual Jewish ceremonies as well as the services and meetings of the Christians. He was the leader of the Judaistic party. Opposing him was Paul, also a strict Jew (in upbringing, at least) and leader of the Christian party in Antioch. Because of his wider experience and education, Paul had greater sympathy with the Gentile groups than had any of the Jerusalem Jews. Each opponent was certain that he was right and both were sure that God's authority was on his side. Argument might lead to a serious split in the Church, but James and Paul both hoped it might be checked.

Perhaps we feel strongly that Paul was right. If so, we must not overlook the fact there was good reason for the Jerusalem Jews to feel anxious. They did not wish to be outnumbered by Gentile converts, for they knew how strong was the idolatry and heathen worship of the non-Jews and how quickly these same Gentiles might forget their new beliefs and even bring into their worship the evil heathen forms of worship they had once practised. The Christian Jews remembered, too, that Jesus and they (his disciples) were Jews, that their beliefs were governed by the Law of Moses, obedience to which was to bring in the Kingdom of God.

Discussion of the Problem

The real question they had to answer seemed to be this—was the new Christian Church part of the old Judaism, tied to the Law of Moses, or was it something entirely new, offering to believers everywhere—Jews and non-Jews—the opportunity of being Christ-followers? In other words—which was important, the baptism of the Holy Spirit or the rite of circumcision? Both sides realised that underlying the question was the fact that if the Law was all-important, Christ had lived and died for no real purpose at all.

In the actual debate Paul has very little to say. After preliminary "disputing" it is Peter who takes charge. It is possible that his meeting with Paul has made clear in his own mind what decision he should take and for whom he should speak. He recounts his own experience with Cornelius, and argues that forcing the Law on the Gentiles would be to make a burden that even they as born Jews could not carry. It was not God's wish that this should be done. The grace of the Lord Jesus was sufficient and the Gospel was universal—for everybody (Gal. ii, 28; Col. iii, 11). Barnabas and Paul then tell of their travels and newly-formed churches. They make it abundantly clear that they did these things under the influence of the Holy Spirit and the power of God. We note here the reversed order of their names; in Jerusalem Barnabas—as their delegate—is still the more important; Paul, even now, is not fully accepted by the Apostles. James and Peter—and perhaps others—appear to be impartial, but there is obviously a small but powerful group against Paul.

The Church Decides

If you have read the verses telling of this debate and have pictured this solemn meeting of serious men, you will have felt something of the atmosphere of challenge between them. You will also experience the great sense of relief when James announces his decision. To everybody's surprise, perhaps, he accepts the arguments and proofs of the experiences of Peter and Paul. One cannot help feeling that he ignores the missionaries, turning rather to the scriptures (Amos ix, 11) to strengthen his points. The Gentiles need *not* accept circumcision. We can imagine the sigh of agreement from all sides. But—there were heathen practices that the Gentiles must give up, so that their lives were clean and pure and fit to offer to Jesus Christ. They must keep three rules:

1. No sharing in any form of heathen worship and sacrifices.
2. No wrong living, especially of the kind found in such heathen worship.
3. No bloodshed of any kind, even the eating of meat from which the blood has not been removed or which has been offered to idols (Lev. xvii, 10; vii, 26).

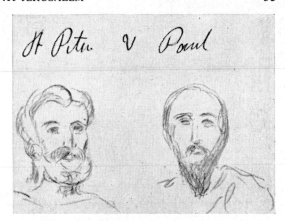

1st Century Catacomb paintings of Peter and Paul. Peter has thick grey hair and beard; Paul's is receding and dark and his beard is pointed.

The missionaries returned to Antioch carrying this decision in a letter from the "Apostles and elders unto the brethren of the Gentiles". They were happy at the success of their meeting in Jerusalem. Judas Barsabas and Silas accompanied them in order to explain further—from the Jerusalem point of view—any matter not clear in the letter. Silas stayed in Antioch.

Closer study of Paul's letters shows that there was still strong feeling on the part of the Jews in Jerusalem. The decision was really a compromise, that is, it was not finally a satisfactory answer for both sides. It made clear that there were still two groups—the Jews and the Gentiles. It was many years before the Jews willingly joined with the Gentiles in worship, for the belief that it was "unclean" for a Jew to mix with—certainly to eat and drink with—a Gentile, was ingrained from their earnest training and could not lightly be thrown on one side. Even in Antioch the separate groups are seen (Gal. ii, 11). In Jerusalem the Christian Church tended to remain strongly Jewish and even anti-Paul (Acts xxi, 20, 21; Rom. xv, 31). Most of the group fled in A.D. 65 when under persecution they found safety in Pella on the east of the Jordan. Pella was a Greek city and there they would meet Hellenist Jews. We wonder how they met and if they joined together under the fear of persecution. Five years later than this, in A.D. 70, as Jesus had foretold, Jerusalem itself was laid waste. But the

A street scene in Jerusalem.

Christian faith had by then spread far and wide
and was something that Roman oppression could
not stamp out.

What happened to Peter?

This is the last time we hear of Peter. Legend
has it that he went to Rome. It is believed that in
about A.D. 64 he gave to Mark the stories of Jesus
that he had been preaching for the past thirty
years; Mark's Gospel certainly reflects the blunt,
impetuous character of Peter. A strong legend
says that in A.D. 42 Peter was in Rome and met
again his old enemy Simon Magus, whose evil
power was still strong. It is said that Peter
was the Bishop of Rome for 25 years, having
founded the Christian church there; he may have
written 1 Peter in about A.D. 63 from Rome.
Imprisoned under Nero's persecutions he is said
to have escaped, but, meeting His Master, asked
"Quo Vadis?" ("Where are you going?") Jesus
said he was going to Rome to be crucified afresh.
Peter returned, and was imprisoned with Paul.
Led out together to die, Peter bade Paul goodbye
and was crucified—as he had asked—head
downwards, unworthy to die as His Master had
died. Over his tomb in Vatican Fields now stands
the great Cathedral of St. Peter.

A Jew reads from a papyrus roll (Book I, p. 32). Perhaps
this is a roll of the prophets or one of Paul's epistles.

The Temple area in modern
Jerusalem. It is Moslem,
not Jewish, but stands on
the site of the ancient
Temple area walked by
Jesus and His disciples.

EXPRESSION WORK

1. Prepare a private conversation between (*a*) Peter and Paul (Gal. ii, 7–17), (*b*) James and Paul (Gal. i, 18, 19).
2. List the points for and against (*a*) barring the Gentiles from, (*b*) accepting them into, the Christian church.
3. Interview Peter.
4. Arrange Chapter xv, 6–29, as a formal debate of the Council of the Palestinian Jews in Jerusalem, inserting your own remarks and arguments where (as in verse 6—"much disputing") they would be useful and relevant. Do not confuse this Council with the Sanhedrin.
5. Read x, 44, 47; xi, 15–18; xv, 8. What have these verses in common? What use did Peter make of them at the Council?
6. Learn Is. lxi, 1. Letter for display Gal. ii, 20, vi, 2a.
7. Sketch Peter *or* James *or* Paul talking to the Council.
8. Explain xv, 10.
9. Why was Peter anxious that the rule of circumcision should not be insisted upon? Why was Paul equally anxious? Gal. iii, 28; Acts xiii, 47, 48; xv, 8–11; xxvi, 16, 17, will help you.
10. As newly accepted Gentiles in one of the Galatian churches, discuss the letter you have received from the Christian Jews in Jerusalem.
11. As Paul, Barnabas, Mark, Silas and Judas Barsabas, discuss the result of the conference in Jerusalem, as you journey to Antioch.
12. Find legends about Peter. Prepare a biography of him.

★　　★　　★

The Council listen to Paul and discuss the problem of accepting the Gentiles into the Christian Church.

CHAPTER 9

THE SECOND MISSIONARY JOURNEY

(xv, 36–xviii, 22)

IT was now A.D. 49. Paul and Barnabas planned to revisit the churches they had set up in Galatia during their previous preaching tour. But there was an unhappy disagreement between them, over John Mark. Barnabas wished to take him, as before, but—still angry at John's leaving them at Perga—Paul refused to let him join them on this second journey (but see 2 Tim. iv, 11). Barnabas therefore took Mark with him and sailed to Cyprus. Paul chose Silas, of whom we have already heard. Silas was also a Roman citizen, his Roman name being Silvanus (1 Thess. i, 1; 2 Thess. i, 1). They travelled in the opposite direction, northwards through Syria and Cilicia (1 Pet. v, 12).

Timothy

Passing *Derbe* they now reached *Lystra*, where, you will recall, lived Timothy. Paul had a great affection for the lad and saw in him a promising preacher and worker for Jesus. Timothy's mother was a Jewess, but his father was a Greek, i.e. a Gentile. But Paul wanted to train him as a missionary and decided it would be better to make Timothy technically a full Jew by having him circumcised. This would make it easier for Timothy to lodge and mingle with the stricter Jews without question; he could eat with them and take part in the synagogue services (1 Tim. i, 18; iv, 14; 2 Tim. 1, 6, cf. Gal. v, 11).

Through Asia Minor

Paul, Silas and Timothy took copies of the letter made at the Council of Jerusalem to each Christian community, but there is no record that they continued to do so with all the new churches. They moved through *Iconium* and *Antioch* in the provinces of Phrygia and Galatia (South Galatia), westwards towards Mysia, intending to enter Bithynia (see map). They reached *TROAS*, an important seaport on the western coast of Asia Minor. Here they must have seen the enormous Greek Theatre where actors of comedy and tragedy attracted vast crowds to watch and cheer the Greek plays. Sometimes the same crowds went to see racing and fighting and even murder in gladiatorial shows. Overlooking the sea was the gymnasium where young Greeks raced naked for the honour of winning the race, their only reward a crown of olive or laurel leaves. Even today we speak of "winning our laurels". There was wrestling and javelin-throwing and discus-throwing. Troas was once called Troy, famed in Greek stories.

Paul Meets Luke

The really important fact for us is that at Troas Paul met the man who was to write his life story. This was Luke, a Greek doctor. The narrative says that Paul saw a man in a vision and that man asked him to go over to Macedonia —to Greece—and so to Europe. Had Paul never obeyed his urge to by-pass Mysia and come down to Troas, despite his intentions of going to Bithynia, the story of his life work—indeed of Christianity—might never have been written; it would certainly have been a different story. Scholars believe that Paul was inspired by his new friend and thought deeply about him and of what he told him. He then decided to cross the Aegean Sea into Greece. Luke appears to have been from the city of Philippi and was probably about to return home. The friendship begun between the two men encouraged Luke to persuade Paul to go with him.

One of the interesting points about Luke's narrative is that every so often there is a passage containing the pronoun "we"; such passages are called "we" sections. They indicate that Luke was actually present at the time of the events he describes (see Introduction). The first of these

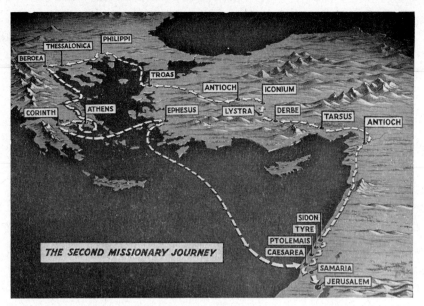

The map shows how Paul and Silas travelled to Europe. Follow the route as you read the chapter.

appears now, immediately after Paul's vision, beginning at verse 10 and continuing to verse 17.

Being a doctor, Luke was able to look after Paul and treat him for his painful complaint—his "thorn in the flesh". One of the most pathetic phrases in Paul's second letter to Timothy is proof of Luke's love and care for him. It is the sentence "Only Luke is with me"—Paul was in prison in Rome and his other friends had fled.

Paul's decision to go with Luke brought Christianity to Europe and speeded its journey to England. Boarding a small trading ship they sailed swiftly across the Hellespont, taking only two days because of the favourable winds; the return journey later on (xx, 6) took five days. *Samothracia* was an island half-way across. They landed at *Neapolis* (Kavalla), a seaport nestling below a hill on which stood a temple to Venus. Eight miles farther on, they reached the Greek city of *PHILIPPI*.

In Philippi

This was now a Roman colony, proudly described by Luke as "the first of the district". It had been begun by Augustus Caesar to mark the beginning of the Roman Empire. It was here that Octavius and Antony had defeated Brutus and Cassius. Today its ruins lie beneath many feet of

This is modern Iconium (Konieh), on the high plateau of Asia Minor.

A scene such as the missionaries might have seen in any Greek city at this time.   Discuss what is going on.

rubble from which have been unearthed tessel-ated pavements, part of the forum and stretches of the famous Via Egnatia, one of the great Roman highways.

Finding no synagogue—there being very few Jews in the locality and not enough to form one —Paul and his companions set out to find a group of Jews. About a mile north of the city, by the riverside, they came across a group—all women. It was a favourable spot for such meet-ings, for there was water for baptism and cere-monial washing. The leader was Lydia. She was a "God-fearer". As a "seller of purple" she was a wealthy woman and had probably come from Thyatira, a town famous for its dyes. The purple dye was most likely obtained by trading with Phoenicia for its sea-shells which, crushed and boiled, gave the necessary liquid. Lydia therefore dealt with royalty and well-to-do people who bought her robes of silk and fine linen (see Luke xvi, 19; xxiii, 53; Mark xv, 17). She offered hospitality to Paul, accepting his message about Jesus and being baptised with all her household.

Imprisoned

The apostles continued their work for some days but soon became aware of a tiresome girl who pestered them with her cries. She possessed "powers of divination" which enabled her to tell fortunes and "look into the future". She was a medium or kind of crystal-gazer; she may even have been able to "throw her voice" as a ventriloquist does. Whatever her powers, she made money for her masters by performing for them. Something in her crazy mind told her that Paul and his friends had greater power and were men of God. Tired of her shouts, Paul turned to her. It was still believed that mad people were possessed of an evil spirit, and, like Jesus years before him, Paul ordered the spirit to come out. He did this "in the name of Jesus". The poor creature, probably feeling that this same Jesus was giving her a clear mind and freedom, felt her madness go and became a healthy-minded girl once more. Naturally the men who employed her and made money out of her gifts, were furious, for they saw at once that she had lost her magical powers and was normal. They forced

Sunset on Thasos N.W. of Samothracia. Perhaps Paul saw it.

Paul and Silas in front of the chiefs of police. The city, like all Roman cities, was governed by a *senate* and two magistrates who were called *praetors*. There were also *lictors* who carried a bundle of rods called *fasces* which were used for punishing culprits and offenders against the law. (The sign of the Italian Fascists in the Second World War was a bundle of these rods.)

The angry men made their charge, but note that it had nothing to do with their own loss; they were too cunning for that. They accused Paul of causing trouble in the city, that he was a Jew trying to win proselytes by teaching beliefs that Romans could not accept. Knowing how the Romans had little thought for anything but law and order, however it was obtained, the men would be making a charge that would readily be accepted. The Jews were evidently unpopular—which was probably why there were so few of them in the city—and the Romans were proud of their Roman citizenship (xvi, 21). Paul and Silas were given summary—instant—punishment. They were stripped and beaten by the *lictors* with their rods. Paul may have wanted to use his rights as a Roman but his cry of " Civis Romanus sum!" would have been drowned by the shouts and his protest was not heard. The two were thrown by the jailer into an underground cell and their feet put into stocks. But undaunted, they sang the Psalms they had learnt as boys and had sung so often in the synagogue.

It was then that the earthquake happened. The account of their escape as the shaking of the earth loosened the stocks and bars of their chains

The Roman jailer is said to have been a centurion, but could have been an ex-service soldier like this (xvi, 29–34).

and flung open the heavy cell door is vivid and exciting (xvi, 25–end). The jailer's life was forfeit if his prisoners escaped; that is why he wanted to kill himself and die honourably. Paul prevented him. Convinced that these were men of God, he and his family believed what Paul had told them and were baptised. The power of the Holy Spirit came upon them and Paul realised that God had accepted them. Note that the jailer's first acts were those of a Christian—to heal and bathe their wounds and then give them food.

There is a "twist" to this story that gives us some amusement. The overbearing magistrates were frightened when they discovered that they

Another scene in the streets of a city. What can you see?

Inside the jail Paul and Silas were put in the stocks, but did not lose heart (xvi, 25). The jail was probably underground and very dark.

had beaten two Roman citizens—worse still, without a trial (xxii, 25; xxv, 11). Paul decided to make an example of them. Very much on his dignity he demanded that the magistrates should "eat humble pie" and come themselves to the cell and publicly request them to leave! We can picture this scene and imagine that many of the watchers laughed heartily at the discomfiture of the cowed magistrates.

Continuing their Journey

Anxious not to cause further unnecessary trouble, and having bidden farewell to Lydia, the apostles left the city. Luke stayed behind, probably to carry on with his work as a doctor; with Timothy he also helped to organise the new church. Paul, Silas and the others went by the fine Via Egnatia to the next cities. On their way they fell in with other travellers—traders, pilgrims, athletes, Roman bodyguards; sometimes wealthy citizens were on their way to Rome itself, riding in their richly draped litters or wagons, attended by slaves with pack-mules of personal property and gifts for their friends. The apostles passed through *Amphipolis* some thirty miles along the road, and another thirty brought them to *Apollonia*. Eventually they arrived at *THESSALONICA* (Salonica). This was the capital of Macedonia, standing on the rising hill overlooking the blue Aegean. It was a "free city", having been honoured by Antony for its help in the Battle of Philippi. It had its own magistrates called "politarchs"; this unusual name has been found in ancient MSS. and confirms Luke's use of it in his account. Paul immediately went to the synagogue and preached, again as was his custom, to the Jews, then to the Greeks. He stayed in the city, probably for a longer period than the three weeks mentioned in the *Acts*. Meanwhile, Timothy had joined them. Money was sent from the church in Philippi (Phil. iv, 16) to assist them in their work. But Paul also had to put to good use his trade of tent-making (1 Thess. ii, 9) and earn enough to pay for his food and lodging.

Paul taught that it was necessary for the Messiah to have suffered, died and risen again from the dead. This, Jesus had done; their Messiah had come and was this Jesus in Whom they should believe. But the Jews grew jealous. They incited a gang of toughs to attack the home of Jason who had given hospitality to Paul and Silas (Rom. xvi, 21). They dragged Jason and some of his friends before the city governors, accusing them of encouraging traitors to Caesar, for, they said, the apostles claimed Jesus as King

The magnificent Parthenon, majestic on its Acropolis (Book II, p. 77). Its carvings are now preserved in the British Museum.

—and there was "no king but Caesar". Note that their charge is a political one, so as to win the favour of the Roman magistrates. To worship Christ was contrary to the worship of Caesar (cf. the dedication at Lystra) and was treason. Jason was released on his promise not to commit treason and on payment of security—"on bail", as we say. 1 Thess. ii, 18 indicates that Paul, who had had to leave so as not to make the situation more difficult for his friends, could not easily return without bringing them again into danger or trouble. There was persecution and serious rioting following this incident (1 Thess. ii, 14–16; iii, 1–5; 2 Thess. i, 6). But the Church he had begun grew fast (1 Thess. i, 8). Timothy was left behind to organise it.

On to Athens

Paul and Silas left in secret and by night. They travelled some forty miles to *Beroea* (Verria), lying 600 ft. above the plain. As usual they went straight into the synagogue where they were better received by both honest open-minded Jews and Greeks of culture and nobility (Acts xvii, 11, 12), who even searched the scriptures to check and prove what Paul was preaching about Jesus. One of Paul's converts was Sopater. But, as we can almost guess by now, it was not long before

jealous Jews of Thessalonica came to the town and made accusations against the apostles and stirred up trouble. Some of the kindly Beroeans helped the two to the harbour where a trading ship took Paul and some of these friends towards the city of ancient fame. Silas and Timothy, who

This amphora (Greek vessel) shows Athene as a warrior.

The altar "To the Unknown God" found at Pergamum.

had come to Beroea to warn Paul, stayed behind to help the elders of the new church in their duties.

For three days the ship coasted along the serried harbours and inlets, passing Olympus—the home of the Greek gods, Ossa and Pelion—giant mountains, Marathon, Thermopylae— renowned in Greek legend and history. Paul must have recalled his learning and the great deeds of the heroes of a past age. In the sunshine and sea air he regained physical strength.

In Athens

ATHENS was the home of heroes, philosophers, orators, poets, teachers, students. No longer powerful, it still retained some of its past glory. Already, Paul could see the magnificent buildings looming on the sky line. There were temples to Zeus, Apollo, Minerva, Dionysus and lesser gods and goddesses; theatres, arenas, amphitheatres, the Tower of the Winds were raised in colonnaded wonder. And crowning them all, white and gold on its Acropolis hill, stood the Parthenon, built in 480 B.C., the temple of Athena, goddess of Wisdom. Many of its

beautiful carvings and friezes are today in the British Museum, preserved from further destruction and ruin. They are now called the Elgin Marbles.

Once in the city, Paul lost no time in wandering about its streets and squares. Wherever he went there were hundreds of statues of gods and goddesses, lifelike in size, but gaudy and unreal in their shrines. He felt that the people must be as powerless as their own gods whom they worshipped in sheer superstition and fear. When it thundered, Zeus was angry; when harvest failed, Demeter was annoyed. The gods had to be appeased. Worship was pagan and false (xvii, 16). The people were blindly obedient and lost to their idols; they bowed down to graven images (Ex. xx, 3–5).

In the great heat of the Mediterranean summer Paul watched the heathen festivals and processions, sacrifices and religious celebrations full of the same superstitious fear of evil spirits. One day, probably still depressed and sad at having had to leave Thessalonica so hurriedly, he was walking through a street when he saw an altar. This was not unusual, except that it was "to an Unknown God", erected at the time of some calamity when they did not know which of the gods had been offended. A similar altar has been unearthed at Pergamum. It set Paul thinking. He had already spoken in the market-place, the civic centre, with its senate house, law courts, town hall and porches. There, as in the Roman forums, men gathered to talk and discuss philosophies and ideals of life, wisdom and goodness. They worshipped Athena, whose forty-feet-high statue, adorned with gold, jewels and ivory, stood in the Parthenon. They were interested in the perfect life, the after-life, the power of the gods and the power of men, government and so on. Paul had argued with the Stoics and the Epicureans. These were philosophers who were searching for answers to the riddles of the universe—"What is Man?" "Why is he here?" They tried to explain their beliefs and to provide patterns for living the perfect life.

Paul and the Philosophers

The *Epicureans* were followers of Epicurus, 300 B.C. They believed that the answers to life's problems lay in happiness at whatever cost.

"Eat, drink and be merry, for tomorrow we die." (1 Cor. xv, 32). The *Stoics* were followers of Zeno, also about 300 B.C. Their name came from *stoa*, the Greek word for porch, where they used to meet. They had a finer attitude towards life than that of the Epicureans. They said gods and men were part of God, therefore they must obey the laws of God, bear their pains and difficulties bravely and well, listen to the voice of conscience and take life calmly. We still use these words. An "epicure" is one who enjoys extravagance in food and living; a "stoic" is one who is indifferent to pain.

These two sects or "schools of thought" as we call them today, were widely different, as can be seen. Both of them listened to Paul courteously, as he spoke to them in the *agora*, their word for market-place. They realised that he was a fluent, educated speaker; they also saw that he was putting forward theories and ideas about life that were new. They were not by any means ready to accept his philosophy; they were too proud and regarded Paul with contempt. Indeed, after hearing him they called him a "babbler", using a Greek slang word which meant "seed-picker"— someone who picks up things fallen from a laden cart. They meant that Paul's knowledge was secondhand and not genuinely his own. Yet they had to admit that when he talked about a "strange god" named Jesus, he seemed to have some authority. Of course, neither sect believed in an after-life; that was quite impossible to accept.

"To an Unknown God"

But it was the custom to give a new speaker every opportunity to say what his philosophy was, in public. So Paul, standing on a platform of rough rock, faced the famous Areopagus, the court or senate responsible for education and religion; its members were scholars and cultured men of high position. The stone benches on which they sat are still to be seen. Gathered around, too, were the ordinary, curious citizens of Athens. Read xvii, 22 ff. These verses give the impression that this was on Ares (Greek) or Mars (Roman) Hill, but it is more likely that it took place in the court of the senate.

Paul adopts the style of the market-place and refers to the known philosophy towards idolatry. The word "superstitious" in verse 22 is misleading, and even sounds rude. What Paul said was really a compliment—"Men of Athens, I see you are rather *religious*." He was thinking of the many altars, statues, shrines and temples he had seen. One of these, he said, was to an Unknown God—of Whom he would tell and so give them new knowledge. Some of his hearers would

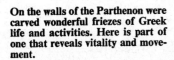

On the walls of the Parthenon were carved wonderful friezes of Greek life and activities. Here is part of one that reveals vitality and movement.

The market-place alive with citizens. What are they discussing?

To Corinth

So far as we know no church was founded in Athens then, though later we read of those who "clave to Paul". In about A.D. 50, Paul left and made his way to *CORINTH*, fifty miles away. Corinth was a busy commercial seaport. Even in those days the canal across the narrow isthmus had been begun. Long before, Alexander the Great, then Julius Caesar had attempted it. Later, Nero—with thousands of captives from Galilee—tried to dig the canal successfully. But it was never finished and Paul must have seen ships moving overland on rollers, making a land journey of four miles to save the long sea route of two hundred miles from gulf to gulf. Corinth was a flourishing Roman centre where Paul was reminded of his boyhood days in Tarsus amongst the Egyptians and Phoenician seamen and boats, traders and caravans, Roman soldiers and Greek athletes. Here he might have a greater chance of success than in Athens. Many of the Jews of the Dispersion lived here, too, and might prove the nucleus of a new group of believers. The lintel of their synagogue has been discovered (Acts xviii. 4).

But here were Greeks, Romans, Egyptians, Jews, lost in their search for new pleasures, money and luxuries, sunk in evil living and selfishness (1 Cor. ix, 24–27). They were superstitious and worshipped gods like Pan, and the Nereids. When not feasting and drinking they were in the theatre "at the games"—the Isthmian Games—where naked athletes raced and wrestled for a laurel wreath and brief fame and chariots hurtled around the arena and gladiators slew one another.

Ancient Corinth, of course, is in ruins. The rocky Acro-Corinth still rises a tawny yellow, 2,000 feet behind excavated sites of temples, baths, squares, wide streets, fountains and triumphal archways. In the centre once stood the temple of Athena; there was another to Aphrodite, goddess of love. Seven huge columns of a temple to Apollo, god of light and power, still stand.

Paul's Work in Corinth

Although he had planned not to stay long (1 Thess. ii, 17, 18) Paul had to find employment for food and lodging. Making his way to the working

perhaps recall that the great philosopher Socrates had spoken to the men of Athens in much the same way, four hundred years before. This, said Paul, was the One True God who created the universe and everything in it. "We also are His offspring", added Paul, quoting from one of their own Stoic philosophers, Aratus, of whom he had learned whilst at school in Tarsus. But this God should not be thought of as an idol of gold or silver or carved stone, as—in their ignorance—their ancestors had done. He did not live in temples made with hands, as did Athena in the Parthenon. He was the Creator and had made all nations; He was now revealed and Paul had seen the One He had sent to be His judge on earth. His people, the Jews, had crucified Him, but God had raised Him from the dead. . . . Paul got no further than this. He was met with roars of scornful laughter and shouts of derision. The crowd dispersed and the senate, perhaps impressed at Paul's obvious sincerity, asked to hear him again.

Paul had failed—not for the first time in his career, and probably not for the last. He had not moved the philosophers of Athens (1 Cor. i, 23, 24; 2 Cor. ii, 1, 2). He did not dream that one day the Parthenon itself would be a Christian church! Of the few converts, two named were Damaris, a woman, and Dionysius, one of the senate. Legend says that Dionysius was later sent by Clement of Rome to France, to preach Christianity. He became Bishop of Paris but was martyred. He is known as St. Denys, the patron saint of France.

quarter of the town, by the dockside and quays, he found a tent-maker, one of his own trade. This was Aquila, a Jew of Pontus who had been sent away from Rome by Emperor Claudius who had become tired of the rioting over "Chrestus" between the Christians and the stricter Jews. Aquila and his wife Priscilla, probably a Roman lady and called Prisca—the family Roman name —in Rom. xvi, 3, allowed Paul to stay with them and listened to his Good News. Aquila in his turn told Paul about Rome and—if tradition is true— about Peter and his work in the great city. Paul decided there and then that one day he, too, would go to Rome and from there speed his message to Spain. Paul must have heard of Britain by now. Claudius himself had been at the taking of Colchester and Roman soldiers had returned from overseas "posting" with their reports of this new land across the sea from Gaul. But for the time being Paul thought only of Rome; he did not know that he would be there in chains as a prisoner. He was not very anxious to begin his preaching in Corinth, after his failure in Athens (1 Cor. ii, 3). But in the workshop and at the weaver's loom he did good work among his new friends and their customers.

Of course, on the sabbath, he attended the synagogue, but the Jews would not believe that the crucified Christ was their promised Messiah. Some of them had probably been in Jerusalem for the Passover in A.D. 29 and vaguely remembered the crucifixion of the "King of the Jews"

now twenty years ago. How could that criminal be the Son of God? In their defiance they cursed Jesus—as had the Jews of Pisidian Antioch.

Paul stood as much as he could of their hostility and disbelief, but in the end his patience vanished. He shook his cloak at them (xviii, 6; cf. Neh. v, 13). He would preach from now on to the Gentiles only. They, at least, would listen to what he had to say. This would anger the Jews, too, for they always hoped that eventually all the God-fearers would become circumcised and accept the Jewish faith; the Jews wanted their membership. Now they were likely to lose them to Paul and his new teaching. Paul, however, struck another blow at them by converting no less a person than their own ruler of the synagogue—Crispus (1 Cor. i, 14). It was natural that the new ruler, Sosthenes, should be his enemy. Then Paul moved into a nearby house, the home of a Roman believer, one Titus (probably Titius) Justus.

One night he had a dream—always accepted in those days as God's way of talking to people— and learned that he was to preach and continue working in Corinth without fear, for the Master was with him. Paul lost no time. Perhaps remembering his failure at Athens, Paul changed his style and method: the Corinthians were a very different kind of people, too. Instead of following a philosophical theme, he went straight to the point of his message about the crucified Christ (1 Cor. ii, 2). His hearers were by no

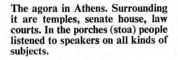
The agora in Athens. Surrounding it are temples, senate house, law courts. In the porches (stoa) people listened to speakers on all kinds of subjects.

The "chorus" of a Greek play. Why are they wearing masks?

means scholarly and cultured; they were neither wise nor noble (1 Cor. i, 26); many were of the most wicked and degraded people to be found in the city (i Cor. vi, 9–11). Paul evidently needed money for his work and was happy to receive from Macedonia gifts that helped tremendously (2 Cor. xi, 8, 9). Silas also rejoined him at this time, having perhaps gone back to Philippi for a short time (Phil. iv, 15). Perhaps it was Silas who brought the gifts. It was necessary that someone should visit the churches as frequently as possible so that they could make sure everything was going well.

Epistle to the Thessalonians

At the time of his successes Paul had a visitor —his beloved Timothy—with good news from

At a Greek seaport. What is happening?

Thessalonica. Unable to do so, but wishing to go there to see for himself and speak once more to his friends, Paul decided to write a letter instead (1 Thess.). This denied the lies of jealous Jews and encouraged the church to live in united friendship. One important point among many is Paul's insistence that since Jesus died and rose again "so shall we all rise again"; there was no sorrow in death (1 Thess. iii, 6; iv, 13, 14; v, 14–22).

This letter is regarded by some scholars as being earlier than the one to the Galatians, i.e. as his first letter to any church at all. The contents certainly seem to show that he looked for an early return of Jesus—the Second Coming— which was expected by all the first Christians. Later, as we see in *Colossians*—and there is some sign in *Galatians*—he regards the Second Coming of Christ as being into the heart of a new believer who has entered into Christ's Kingdom on earth. We have his letters to this day and if you have looked up the references given you, you will have read part of them already. The letter to the *Thessalonians* and the one to the *Galatians* form the beginnings of the New Testament, for as yet none of the Gospels has been written (Book III, Introduction). Silas was present when Paul wrote this letter and probably penned it on the papyrus sheets as Paul dictated it, for Paul's eyes, as we believe, were too weak for him to write long letters (1 Thess. i, 1). Later, Paul sent another letter to this church, encouraging it to continue in its work, not to worry about the Second Coming of Jesus but to carry on with their duties. He reminded them to be busy bodies but not busybodies! (2 Thess. i, 3, 4; ii, 2; iii, 7–11).

The Church at Corinth

Paul stayed at Corinth, forming a church amongst the poorest Gentiles; he trained leaders to carry on with the duties involved so that the church would run smoothly. He also introduced to them the service of the Lord's Supper (Book III). It was not a united church; there was considerable disagreement and disorder and even opposition to Paul himself. But it was large and there was evidence of "speaking with tongues", so Paul felt that the Holy Spirit was working for him. He stayed for some eighteen months and

1. **Theatre**—drama, political assemblies.
2. **Odeon**—music and plays.
3. **Glauke**—a fountain.
4. **Museum**—relics of the city.
5. **Temple of Apollo.**
6. **Julian Basilica**—Roman law courts.
7. **Sanctuary of Apollo.**
8. **Roman shops** (1 Cor. x, 25).
9. **Gateway to road** (xviii, 4).
10. **Peirene**—a reservoir.
11. **East building.**
12. **Bema**—speaker's platform (xviii, 12–17).
13. **Shops.**
14. **Stoa**—porches.
15. **South Building**—Basilica.

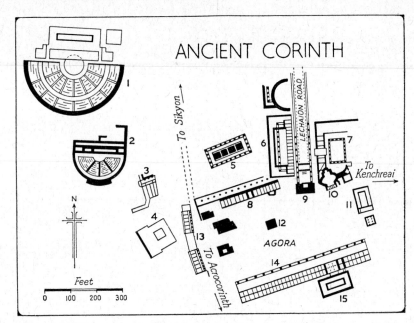

ANCIENT CORINTH

then in early A.D. 52 decided that he must return to Antioch and thence to Jerusalem.

Before he could do so, however, he was brought by a mass gathering of jealous Jews before the new Roman pro-consul of Achaia, Gallio. An inscription about Gallio, dated A.D. 52, has been found at Delphi, and this has helped to date this period with accuracy. Gallio was brother to Seneca, the Roman philosopher and tutor to Nero. Seneca once said, "So live with men as if God saw; so speak with God as if men were listening." This ideal of life is strangely like Paul's.

Seated at the judgment seat in the Basilica or Judgment Hall, Gallio sensed the jealousy of the Jews and saw through their vague charges that he was preaching a new religion which by Roman law he was not allowed to do. He told them that it was not his business to judge matters of their own law and religion; they must deal with such things themselves. As far as he could see Paul was not preaching treason against Rome. Christianity could continue if it would. Seeing that Gallio had snubbed the Jews (xviii, 14–16) the Greeks turned on the new synagogue ruler Sosthenes and beat him; Gallio ignored this, too.

Paul Leaves Corinth

With Aquila and Priscilla, Paul sailed for Syria, pausing at *Cenchraea*, the eastern port of Corinth lying between two horns of land on the end of which stood temples—one to Aphrodite, the other to Isis. Here Paul had his head shaved to indicate that he had taken a vow (Num. vi). The ship sailed across the bay passing a rock on which stood a huge statue of Poseidon (Roman Neptune), god of the sea, bearing his dolphin and trident. Arriving at *Ephesus*, Aquila and Priscilla stayed, for they had planned to live there. Paul had time to speak but once in the synagogue, for, having found another ship and anxious to complete his journey, he sailed across the eastern Mediterranean to the Roman seaport of *Caesarea*. He promised to revisit Ephesus at some future opportunity (xviii, 21). From Caesarea he travelled southwards to *Jerusalem*. Scholars tell us that the "church" in verse 22 was at Jerusalem, where, as he had taken the vow at Cenchraea, he could redeem (buy back) his vow by offering on the Temple altar the hair that had grown during the previous month. He may have had a cold reception from the Jews in Jerusalem, but in *Antioch* was certainly received joyfully.

His arrival in Antioch ended his Second

Weaving on a vertical loom as Aquila might have done.

Missionary Journey in Greece. The rest of Acts xviii begins the Third Journey—this time into Asia.

EXPRESSION WORK

1. Read Acts viii, 9; xiii, 6; xvi, 16. Say what you can of sorcery,
   or
   Write a radio script of the healing of the fortune-teller.
2. Write a "quarrel scene" between Paul and Barnabas, over John Mark. Silas might act as "peacemaker".
3. As Timothy, write home telling of your adventures,
   or
   As Paul, write to your friends about meeting Luke at Troas,
   or
   As Luke, write home to say you have met Paul and will bring him to Philippi,
   or
   As Lydia, write to friends in Thyatira about Paul's work.
4. Make a strip cartoon to tell the story of the escape from prison of Paul and Silas,
   or
   Draw the part of the story that is most vivid in your mind.
5. Interview one or all of the following: Lydia, Jason, the jailer, the magistrates, Dionysius, Aquila and Priscilla.

6. What were some of Paul's thoughts (*a*) before, (*b*) after, entering Athens?
   or
   Divide into groups of Stoics and Epicureans and discuss your "philosophy of life". (This is a difficult exercise and will need preparation.)
7. Make a frieze or model of the Second Journey, in the style of that for the First Journey.
8. Learn 1 Thess. iii, 13, 14. Learn the words of Seneca, writing out what you think is their exact meaning.
9. What special difficulties did Paul have to face in Athens? What advantages did he find? Why did he seem to fail there? Was it a complete failure or do you consider that two converts were worth his efforts?
10. Describe or act Paul's first meeting with Aquila and Priscilla. What did they talk about? How did Paul regain his better spirits after being so unhappy about Athens?
11. Rewrite Paul's speech in modern language. Compare it with a version made by a modern writer. Speak it to the class as Paul might have done to the Areopagus.
12. The following references give names and types of members of the church at Corinth. Find these and list them: 1 Cor. i, 26 ff.; vii, 20–24; xii, 13; i, 14, 16; i, 11; Rom. xvi, 1 ff., 23. See if you can find others to add to this list.

Where 20,000 people shouted, "Great is Diana of the Ephesians!"

CHAPTER 10

THE THIRD MISSIONARY JOURNEY

(xviii, 23–xxi, 17)

AFTER a few months, Paul prepared to set out once again. The roads were once more hard after the winter rains had softened them into muddy tracks. He passed through Galatia and Phrygia, revisiting the churches established on his first mission. He had promised to return to *EPHESUS* and hastened on to do so. In the meantime, a new leader, "eloquent and learned", had arisen at Ephesus. This was Apollos. He had already been in Corinth when Paul was there (1 Cor. i, 12). Coming originally from Alexandria he knew something of the message of John the Baptist but little of Jesus; his preaching therefore lacked the conviction that came from the acceptance of Christ as the Messiah. He did not possess the power of the Holy Spirit and knew nothing of Christian baptism. Apollos was advised to go to Ephesus so that he could receive instruction and guidance from Paul. Aquila and Priscilla who had by now settled in Ephesus, carrying on with their craft of tent-making, gave Apollos considerable help; they probably told Luke about him, too. Apollos returned to Corinth where he had many followers, some of them preferring his preaching to that of Paul.

Travelling with Paul at this time were Timothy and Titus, young preachers in training. The city was a great commercial and governing centre. With six other fine cities not far from it, it made the "seven churches" of Rev. i, 9–iii, 22. But it was also a pagan city, given over to the worship of the goddess Artemis (Diana) whose huge temple was the glory of Ephesus and once one of the seven wonders of the world. It was built in 330 B.C. Part of its ruins are now in the British Museum; the rest lie beneath mosquito-infested stagnant swamps. It was shown on the coins of the Greeks, with the beautiful Diana represented with her deer or with lions crouching to spring. But the actual image was not that of a beautiful goddess familiar to us in pictures of the moon goddess or huntress of Greek stories. It was originally a rough black lump of rock (a meteorite) that had fallen from the skies and which the superstitious Ephesians had believed had come from heaven itself, sent by Jupiter. Some sources tell us that it was a roughly-carved piece of wood resembling a woman. Its shrine was curtained and surrounded by a hundred columns of shining jasper, each on a marble base. The roof of the temple was painted in red and gold. Priests, priestesses and musicians served in the temple, whilst dancers and even acrobats performed and magicians and sorcerers practised their arts. The people themselves were ridden with fear of these servants of the goddess, and were in greater fear of Artemis herself (Eph. vi, 12).

Paul and the Ephesians

But Paul found many Ephesians who were looking for something better in life than fear and superstition. They, too, had a faith, but only that of John the Baptist; they were still hoping for the promised Messiah and had never heard of the power of the Holy Spirit (Acts xix, 2 ff.). So Paul taught them about Jesus and Pentecost and the power of the Spirit came upon them even as he blessed them.

Naturally, he went to the Jewish synagogue. The Jews simply would not accept the crucified Messiah. So Paul took over a kind of lecture room, probably in the local gymnasium, with the help of a teacher named Tyrannus. Normal school hours were from sunrise until 11 a.m. after which it was too hot for work. So Paul had to use the hall from the fifth to the tenth hour, the hottest period of the day from 11 a.m. until just before sunset, after which it would be required again by the owners for educational work in the cool evening. For two years Paul preached in this hall (1 Cor. xvi, 6, 8; 2 Cor. i, 15, 16).

THE THIRD
MISSIONARY
JOURNEY

MILES
0   50   100   150   200

Paul's Third Journey enabled him
to revisit his earlier churches where
he praised, reproved and encouraged the members to continue in
their faith.

His Good News was simple and direct—"repen-
tance towards God and faith towards our Lord
Jesus Christ". He seems at this period to have
worked several miracles through the great faith
the people had in Jesus. Because of this power
the seven sons of Sceva, a Jew and a chief priest,
tried to copy Paul, believing that they had only
to use the words "Jesus" and "Paul" for this
strange magic to be theirs. But they did not
succeed. Those who heard of their failure believed
all the more firmly in what Paul was preaching,
for they saw for themselves that he had a power
no others could possess—and this power came
from Jesus Christ.

"Great is Diana of the Ephesians!"

Paul's teaching was clear and the Ephesians
had long wanted such a religion. They were tired
and disgusted at the heathen rites and witchcraft
of the false gods, and gave up their idolatry in
order to accept the new teaching. Even the sorcerers, seeing the wrong they were doing and
realising the foolishness of their so-called magic,
brought their scrolls of spells, magical formulae
and charms into the market-place. There they
had an enormous bonfire, the value of the
"books" (they were really papyrus rolls) being

fifty thousand pieces of silver; it is difficult to
assess this in present-day money, but it would
not be less than £5,000. One inscription they did
not destroy, for on a block of marble found at
Ephesus we read one of their superstitions—"If
the bird is flying from right to left, then whether
it rises or settles out of sight, it is unlucky".

But Paul's success was not complete. It was
now May, A.D. 55, and the pagan spring festivals
were being held. May 24th was the day of
Artemis. Diana was her Roman name. In Book

The theatre at Ephesus was like this.

The goddess Diana (Artemis). Find all you can about her.

II you will have read how the god Marduk was brought through the city of Babylon in processions of rejoicing. It was a common celebration in eastern countries. Now, the Greek goddess Artemis, goddess of fertility, the "Great Mother", was to be honoured. Her statue was to be drawn by deer through the city streets, the people singing and chanting hymns of praise and falling down in worship. The city was packed with visitors and pilgrims all bent on their search for good luck and blessing on their crops and journeys and homes. Usually, the silversmiths and other craftsmen did an enormous trade in their little figurines and statuettes of Diana in silver, terra-cotta and wood; the people bought these as souvenirs and charms. Demetrius was one of these craftsmen. Since Paul came with his new religion, Demetrius had seen his trade diminish; people who believed in this Jesus had no further use for charms and images. He was losing trade; and Diana was being despised. Roused to anger, the smiths and their workmen

forced two friends of Paul—Gaius and Aristarchus (Col. iv, 10; Phile. 24)—into the auditorium or amphitheatre which held over 20,000 people. They had tried to find Paul but by now Aquila had persuaded him to leave (Rom. xvi, 3, 4).

Paul had wanted to face the crowd, but he was advised not to do so by the presiding governors or Asiarchs, as they were called. They were the rulers of the provinces of Asia which was then a Roman province in the west of Asia Minor. They may have favoured Paul as an educated preacher and a Roman, but they also wanted to prevent trouble. The mob—who for the most part did not know what or why they were shouting—chanted their slogan unintelligently for two whole hours! They would not listen to Alexander, a Jew (2 Tim. iv, 14), but drowned his voice in their cry of "Great is Artemis (Diana) of the Ephesians". It was not until the "town clerk" or mayor—a city official—spoke sternly to them that they calmed down, no doubt quite exhausted and glad of the opportunity to be quiet and go home. He reminded them that Ephesus was "sacristan" or temple-keeper of Diana; this was a title of honour given to those who worshipped Caesar. Paul and his friends had done nothing against the city and had not robbed the temple (Rom. ii, 22). Their rioting might be questioned by Rome and as a result

A Roman aqueduct. What was its purpose?

Once a battlefield (42 B.C.) the Plain of Philippi is now a swamp.

they might lose their privilege of being a "free city" (Acts xix, 38; 1 Cor. iv, 13). If Demetrius wished to make a charge he could do so in the usual courts of law.

The Jews were probably glad that the riot had not turned against them, as it might easily have done once the rioters had realised that Paul was a Jew. The fact that he was a Christian Jew would have escaped them.

The Epistle to the Corinthians

At this time Apollos returned from Corinth (1 Cor. xvi, 12, 17) with disquietening news that there was disunity and backsliding in the church there. Many of the members had returned to their former heathen beliefs and ways of living; others were anxious because their new beliefs were not being fulfilled. They had looked for an early Second Coming of Jesus and were getting tired of waiting. Paul decided to write to them. "I hear sad things of you," he said, "and you are not ashamed." He told them he now knew of their wickedness, drunkenness, even feasting at the Lord's Supper; he was perplexed at their return to idolatry. He knew there were divisions amongst them. Some followed him, others Apollos. What did it matter? He had planted the seed, Apollos had watered it, but God had made it grow—and this meant that they had got to work together for full success of the church. His letter is forceful and to the point throughout. The well-known Ch. xiii sums up his teaching of the power of Jesus' love.

Titus took Paul's letter to Corinth and Paul went on to *Troas* (2 Cor. ii, 12; vii, 5-7) accompanied by Luke. Paul was too ill to preach (2 Cor. i, 8; iv, 7), so the two travelled through *Macedonia* and other parts of Greece. It is probable that Paul visited *Corinth* during this time (2 Cor. ii, 1; xiii, 1 ff.). He was anxious at further news of the church and depressed at his "thorn in the flesh" (2 Cor. i, 8; iv, 7 ff.; xii, 7, 9). Titus returned to *Philippi* to tell him more of the quarrels (2 Cor. vii, 6). The majority were loyal to Paul and this gave him great joy. But those who were not were being urged on by Jews from Jerusalem and were plotting against him, his requests for money and his teaching. They even said he was a coward; this was a charge no one could justifiably make against a man who had dared and suffered as had Paul. He rose to the occasion and promptly wrote another letter— the latter part of 2 Cor.—in bold, almost threatening language full of sensitive anger. Begin reading it at Ch. x. In xi, 24–28, he lists more than sufficient evidence that he was no coward.

Timothy now arrived and Titus took this letter to Corinth. Later, Paul and Timothy themselves went (xx, 2) to refute the mean charges made against him. Scholars tell us that the two epistles as we have them are really made up of fragments of four.

Epistle to the Romans

Whilst he was at *Corinth*, Paul sent a letter to the church in Rome. It was written down for

An orator addresses the Assembly as Paul may have done.

Chios, in the Aegean Sea, where Paul paused on his return journey.

him by Tertius (xx, 1 ff.; Rom. xv, 25). In Rome was a group of Christians, the beginnings of a Christian church possibly started by Peter in the heart of the Roman Empire. A good introduction to the letter is to read Ch. vii, iii, xii, in that order; these chapters tell of Paul's guidance in "getting right with God" (cf. Luke xvii, 9–14). He underlines and explains the difference between the power of faith in Jesus and the acceptance of the Jewish Law and Tradition, and is reminiscent of his letter to the Galatians. The following references will help you to see that he showed them how their faith in Jesus would enable them to lead the right kind of life, however difficult they found it—viii, 38, 39; vii, 21; v, 3, 4. Read also iii, 24–27; viii, 35. He told them that he hoped to visit them in person, to preach what he was then writing—i, 14, 15; xv, 24, 25, 30, 33. Ch. xvi reveals Paul's wonderful capacity for friendship.

Continuing the Work

Despite criticisms he continued to collect money to send to the church in Jerusalem (1 Cor. xvi, 1–4; 2 Cor. viii; Rom. xv, 26). After three months he seems to have decided to return, perhaps in one of the pilgrim ships bearing hundreds of Jews of the Dispersion to Caesarea on their way to Jerusalem to keep Passover. But he was warned of a plot by the jealous Jews to kill him, so he changed his plans and went overland through Macedonia, spending Passover in *Philippi* (1 Cor. v, 7).

In *Troas* once more—about A.D. 56—he met the members of his party. There were Sopater from Beroea, Aristarchus from Thessalonica, Luke from Philippi, Gaius from Derbe, Timothy from Lystra, Tychicus and Trophimus from

Kalymnos lies between Samos and Coos. Paul saw these hills.

The ruins of the Temple of Apollo at Miletus where Paul bade good-bye to his Ephesian friends.

Ephesus. These were all bringing gifts and money for Jerusalem. Note that the "we" passages begin again at xx, 5–15, indicating that Luke is once again with Paul. Of course, he may have been there before, but is certainly with Paul on these occasions. In xx, 7, we read that the company met to "break bread" in remembrance of the Lord's death (Book III). This would be in a private house on the evening before the sabbath day. The meeting followed an order of service not unlike that of the synagogue—Prayer (cf. 1 Cor. xiv, 16) and Praise (Eph. v, 19; Rom. xiii, 11, 12), then a Reading—from the Greek Septuagint, LXX—followed by an explanation of how

The Colossus at Rhodes represented Apollo, god of light and music. Ships passed between its legs (p. 77).

its teachings bore out the life and work of Jesus. On this occasion Paul spoke well into the early hours of the morning. It is not surprising that Eutychus should fall drowsily from his perch at the window of the upper room. Paul revived him.

Homeward Bound

We next find Paul walking alone the twelve miles to *Assos*, probably to think and prepare for his immediate return to Jerusalem. There had already been a definite plot against his life and he knew perfectly well that he was in danger the nearer he moved towards the city. He rejoined the company who had gone by sea. Assos stood high on a hill overlooking the blue Aegean Sea. Ruins show that in Paul's day there was a temple to Athena and a fine agora or market-place and also a Roman bath. The whole company then sailed on to *Mitylene* taking advantage of the strong breezes that blew by day and dropped by night. Then to *Chios, Samos*, probably "tarrying at *Trogyllium*"; then they arrived at *Miletus*. Paul had planned to by-pass Ephesus because of his wish to hurry to Jerusalem for Pentecost; it is possible, too, that he did not want to create fresh trouble in the city by showing himself so soon after his hasty exit. But not wishing the loyal Ephesians to feel he was neglecting them, he sent for the elders of the church. Their journey of twenty-five miles across the coastal mountains and probably a sea-crossing caused a delay of three or four days. Whilst the sailors prepared the boat for the next run, the Ephesians talked with Paul on the sandy shore.

In his farewell speech to them Paul used his personal experiences as an example and begged them to be likewise diligent and conscientious in their work against all opposition from within the church (xx, 30; 1 Tim. i, 3–7). In xx, 35, is a saying not recorded in the Gospels—which, we must remember, were not yet written—though to most people so familiar that they would say it was. Paul's use of it shows that the sayings of Jesus were already being used in the churches. So it was, in the shadow of the temple to Apollo and within a short distance of the huge Roman theatre with its special seats "Reserved for Jews and God-fearers", that Paul bade a sad goodbye to his Ephesian friends. Among these were surely Aquila and Priscilla. They "sorrowed most of all for the words which he spake, that they should see his face no more". Sad at heart, the elders escorted Paul down the Sacred Way to the seashore and watched the ship bear away their beloved preacher. No doubt Paul raised his hand high in blessing on them as the boat sped on and away from the shore and they could see him no more.

Swift Return

The ship made a fast run by *Coos* and *Rhodes* —where the 112-feet-high bronze Colossus (Apollo), once one of the Seven Wonders of the World, now lay in pieces across the harbour entrance. It had been thrown down by an earthquake as early as 224 B.C. Nine hundred years later it was sold to the Saracens for scrap metal!

Following the course taken for this return journey you will see that it kept closely to the coast, which indicates that the boat was a coasting vessel. At *Patara* they boarded a larger trading ship and made across the eastern Mediterranean, passing the south-western tip of Cyprus, towards Phoenicia, finally landing at *Tyre*. Here the cargo took seven days to unload and Paul's friends of the seaport begged him not to continue to Jerusalem, for they felt it would be dangerous for him to do so. Despite their

These forbidding rocks lie off the island of Rhodes.

prayers and pleadings, Paul, Luke and the others boarded the ship again and it sailed down the coast to *Ptolemais* (Acre). Here they landed and next day walked the thirty miles to *Caesarea*. This was the Roman political capital of Palestine and the residence of the Roman procurators. It had been built by Herod the Great in honour of Augustus Caesar; there was a magnificent harbour, and fine streets and subways threaded the city. Temples of marble and lofty palaces indicated the wealth and luxury to be found there.

A Corinthian winejug that has been dug up at Rhodes. Paul saw and used many like it when he stayed in Corinth.

This camel train moving along the shore of N. Palestine is led, according to tradition, by a donkey.

Cut in the hillside was a hippodrome called an "odeon". It held twenty thousand people. Sea-water could be flooded into the theatre arena so that sea-battles, races and displays could be shown.

Here, however, was a Christian community. We remember it was here that Peter had baptised Cornelius and that Philip the Evangelist had his home. It was with Philip that Paul now stayed. Whilst in Caesarea they met Agabus, a prophet of Judaea, who foretold danger to Paul if he went to Jerusalem. Note that Agabus revived the tradition of the Old Testament prophets who illustrated their prophecies by something the people could see. He used Paul's girdle to signify that Paul would be bound hand and foot in Jerusalem (cf. Jer. xiii, 1–11). But Paul was "willing to die at Jerusalem". His Master had once "set His face steadfastly to go to Jerusalem" and so would he (Rom. xv, 25–32). So

his friends prepared the pack-mules and donkeys —to carry them and the heavy chest of coins and jewels collected for the relief fund in Jerusalem— and started for the city. They had only two days if they were to arrive in time for Pentecost and there was no time to walk. Accompanying them was an "early disciple" of the first persecutions; this was a Greek Jew named Mnason. He probably gave Paul hospitality whilst he was in *Jerusalem*. Paul may also have stayed with his sister (xxiii, 16).

EXPRESSION WORK

1. Arrange a conversation between Aquila and Apollos (see 1 Cor. iii, 5; xvi, 12; i, 10–iv, 21; cf. 2 Cor. x, 7).
2. Write a newspaper report on "The Bonfire at Ephesus".
3. Prepare a radio commentary on, *or*, as a visitor describe, the Procession of Diana.
4. Draw part of the procession, *or* the mob in the amphitheatre.
5. Learn for choral verse-speaking 1 Cor. xiii.
6. Prepare as a dramatic reading, for presentation in a Morning Assembly, xix, 20–41.
7. As Paul, "think aloud" as you walk to Assos.
8. Make a frieze or model the Third Missionary Journey.
9. As elders of the Ephesian church, report back to your members and tell them what happened at Miletus.
10. Find all you can about Caesarea. Give a talk, with illustrations.
11. Who were: Agabus, Demetrius, Jason, Eutychus?
12. Learn Eph. vi, 10–18. Draw a Roman soldier to illustrate the verses.

Where once stood the ancient city of Tyre.

CHAPTER 11

PAUL IN JERUSALEM

(xxi, 17–xxiii)

AS always at times of great feasts, Jerusalem was thronged with pilgrims. Thousands of them had come for Pentecost from all parts of the Roman Empire. Some of them were from far-away cities in which Paul had preached and where he had been hindered and even badly treated by the jealous Jews. They came from Pisidian Antioch, Iconium, Athens, Corinth . . . Some of them had even followed Paul for the very purpose of stirring up trouble in those cities. They hated Paul for opening the door of the Christian faith to the Gentiles and they hated him because—in their eyes—he was a traitor to his own Jewish faith.

In the Temple Court

At first welcomed—"they glorified God"—Paul faced the Jews of the Jerusalem church now under James. We do not know what happened to the original disciples; they must have been scattered throughout the empire and beyond, taking the story of Jesus with them. It is believed, for instance, that Thomas went to India, Peter was in Rome, and later, Mark went to Alexandria. Paul presented the money and gifts he had brought and recounted his adventures and experiences. But instead of real joy at the vast growth of the church there was some coldness and even antagonism towards him. Paul was made to feel that he had gone too far; the Christian Jews of Jerusalem obviously did not approve of his methods. Now that he was in Jerusalem he must behave like a good Jew and join in the Temple rites and sacrifices. In fact, it would be a good idea to do this publicly by paying the expenses into the Temple treasury of four men then under a vow. (It appears from this that Paul was now wealthy; we do not know where he obtained his money, but he was able later to rent a house, whereas we have seen that he had to work at tent-making for his living.)

Paul agreed to this public act and had his own head shaved, joining in the vow. On the last of the twelve days' attendance at the Temple he was recognized by some of his Asian (Ephesian) enemies. He and a Gentile friend, Trophimus, were in the Court of the Gentiles. You will remember that this was the only part of the Temple precincts in which a Gentile was allowed. A barrier wall of marble stretched across the entrance to the next court. On it were the words, "No foreigner may enter within the screen and enclosure round the Holy Place. Whosoever is caught so trespassing will himself be the cause of death overtaking him" (Book II, p. 88). The angry Ephesians jumped to the conclusion that Paul had so far defied the ban on Gentiles as to take Trophimus beyond the warning inscription. They shouted that he had already preached against Moses and the Law and the Temple, and now he had deliberately desecrated the Temple itself (cf. xxiv, 6).

Paul was dragged beyond the Beautiful Gate and out of the Temple courts. His enemies were bent on stoning him to death outside the city walls, for breaking their Jewish law. He was dramatically rescued by the Roman garrison of the Castle of Antonia which overlooked the Temple. The legionaries were always on the look-out for disturbances during feast times. From time to time there were rebellions and uprisings. One was under Judas, in Galilee, in A.D. 7. Another followed, led by his two sons. A Messianic rising took place under Theudas who led his followers towards Jordan to cross as Moses had done at the Red Sea; this was in A.D. 44, wrongly dated by Luke in v, 36. There were wars between the Samaritans and the Zealots. One section of the Zealots were called the "Sicarii" or "dagger-men" or the "Assassins". These were anxious to overthrow Roman rule at any cost. Not long before this incident involving

The present Temple area on the site of Herod's Temple.

Paul, an Egyptian had gathered his followers on the Mount of Olives, promising that the walls of Jerusalem would fall like those of Jericho; they would then enter the city and pillage it. They were, however, scattered by the Roman soldiers; four hundred were killed and two hundred captured. The Egyptian leader escaped. When Paul was taken Claudias Lysias believed that he had at last captured the Egyptian! (xxi, 38). Lysias was a *chiliarch*, commander of a *cohort* of 600 men (ten cohorts made a *legion*). His duties were those of a magistrate and commander combined, so he was really a *tribune* or military governor. He was surprised to hear Paul speak to him in Greek.

Protected but bound in chains, Paul offered to speak to the mob. Lysias welcomed any effort to stop rioting and recognised Paul as obviously a brave and educated man. Paul held them for a time in their own Hebrew tongue—he may even have spoken Aramaic—and told them of his conversion on the Damascus road when actually on his way as a zealous Jew to persecute the Nazarenes. They listened until he reached the point that he was sent by Jesus "far hence unto the Gentiles". Again furious that he should make the Gentiles equal to themselves the Jews rose at him. "Away with him! It is not fit that he should live!" Some of their fathers had cried "Crucify Him!" against their Lord. Lysias had to thrust Paul up the steps into the stronghold for safety.

But Lysias was still worried at the possible consequence of Paul's speech. Without further questioning he gave the customary orders to strip and scourge the prisoner to make sure that he would confess. It was then that Paul claimed his rights as a Roman citizen; there was no point in undergoing punishment that was then unnecessary. Note the difference between their "freedoms". Lysias had bought his—hence the "Claudius", his Emperor's name; Paul was "freeborn". Lysias was, of course, most anxious at his personal responsibility and was greatly relieved that he had, in the nick of time, avoided the dreadful crime of punishing a Roman citizen! Paul's chains were removed.

Paul and the Sanhedrin

Next day Paul met the Sanhedrin, or Council of the Jews, Lysias being hopeful that such a meeting would solve his problem. The Council had seen Paul before; he had been a student under Gamaliel, who himself may have gazed in perplexity on his wilful ex-pupil. They were all set against him; they were like the Council that had condemned Jesus thirty years before. Even Ananias the High Priest so far forgot himself as

A bronze statuette of Nero in armour.

to order Paul to be struck; he was to meet his death soon after, at the hands of the Zealots. Paul had called him a "whited wall"—strongly reminiscent of the words of Jesus (Matt. xxiii, 27). Note how cleverly Paul divided the seventy amongst themselves and diverted attention from himself. He asserted his loyal Jewish beliefs as a Pharisee and said he had been called before them because of his belief in the resurrection of the dead. This created an uproar as the Sadducees and Pharisees shouted and argued over the resurrection and existence of angels. The Pharisees supported Paul, agreeing that if an angel had spoken to him they could not fight against God; the Sadducees denied such things. Paul was then taken to the Roman cells. That night he dreamed that His Master told him to be of good cheer, for, as in Jerusalem, so was he to bear witness for Him—in Rome!

Escape from Jerusalem

You will recall that Paul had a sister who had married into a high-priestly family and lived in Jerusalem. Her son, Paul's nephew, now came to the prison to warn Paul not to attend the Sanhedrin again, for a group of forty men had plotted to kill him. The Jews knew they could not get at Paul in the Castle, therefore they would murder him with the full knowledge—and consent—of the priests in the Council. Lysias was told. He was not very happy about it, for he had not only to protect Paul as a Roman citizen but also to maintain law and order. He therefore decided to send Paul to headquarters in Caesarea, where Felix the Governor (procurator) would take him in charge.

So Paul was put in the charge of two centurions and two hundred footsoldiers, two hundred spearmen and "beasts" (mules) to bear him. This seems an unusually large escort, but there was danger of an ambush from Paul's enemies and also from brigands and robbers on the way. Lysias was taking no chances. They travelled by night, leaving at nine o'clock, and journeyed the thirty-five miles to Antipatris. Here, on the edge of the plain and beyond the mountainous hideouts of possible murderers, the footsoldiers and spearmen left to return to Jerusalem. Paul was taken the remaining thirty miles

The "parting of the ways" on the Damascus road.

to the coast in the care of the horsemen. He was put into yet another prison to await trial. Read the covering letter sent by Lysias and compare its contents with what actually happened; you can see how he distorts the facts to his own advantage (cf. xxii, 23–29, and xxiii, 26–30).

Paul was to stay in his prison in Herod the Great's palace, then the residence of the Governor, for two whole years. Cilicia, his home province, was—with Syria—under the Legate, who was Felix's superior military governor. As the Legate's deputy Felix could, therefore, try Paul.

Hill country through which Paul journeyed to Caesarea.

A Roman gateway like this guarded the entrance to each city.

Roman spearmen accompanied Paul part of the way to Caesarea.

Felix, we are told, was a cruel, wicked procurator; he had enforced his control of Judaea by crucifixion and murder. But Paul escaped torture and scourging because, although a Jew, he could claim Roman rights.

EXPRESSION WORK

1. As a group of Christian Jews in Jerusalem, discuss Paul's work and lay a plan of action (a) before Paul arrives, (b) with Paul present.
2. Plot the arrest of Paul.
3. Dramatise the rescue of Paul by Claudius Lysias.
4. What do you consider to be the two main reasons for the Jews' anger towards Paul?
5. Account for the difference between the freedoms of Paul and Lysias.
6. Draw Paul before the Sanhedrin.
7. Prepare a dialogue between Gamaliel and his ex-pupil Paul.
8. As Paul's nephew, bring news of the plot to murder your uncle.
9. Describe the journey of Paul and his escort to (a) Antipatris, (b) the rest of the way to Caesarea.
10. Draw a strip cartoon or Poor Man's Bible illustration of the events in this chapter.
11. How does Claudius Lysias alter the real facts in his report to Felix? Why does he do this? What do you think about it?
12. Letter 1 Cor. xvi, 13, for classroom display,
    or
    Interview: Trophimus, one of the Ephesians, the Centurion.

The footsoldiers included slingers (see also Book I, p. 79).

At Caesarea Paul would see many a Roman galley.

CHAPTER 12

PAUL AND THE ROMAN GOVERNORS

(xxiv–xxvi)

FIVE days after his arrival in Caesarea, Paul was brought before the Governor's tribunal or court. Paul's accusers, furious that he had slipped through their fingers, came from Jerusalem to make their charges. Ananias the High Priest, still smarting at Paul's remark, was there, and Tertullus the lawyer put the case against Paul. It is easy to see how he tries to curry favour with Felix (xxiv, 2) and puts the blame on Lysias but for whom the Sanhedrin might have dealt with Paul. The accusation is that Paul is a rebel, a troublemaker and a ringleader of the Nazarenes; further, he is a profaner of the Temple. It would be better to get rid of him before further rioting took place because of him.

Paul and Felix

Felix has the level-headed sense of justice we saw in Pontius Pilate (Book III) and does not allow himself to be persuaded against Lysias by Tertullus. He gives Paul the opportunity of defending himself. Paul denies the charges and adds that there is no proof of them even if he had done the things of which he is accused. He asks where are his false accusers, the Ephesians, and explains why he was in the Temple and how Lysias had protected him. His "crime" is his belief in His Master and in the resurrection; this, he says, is what the Sadducees regard as "wrong-doing".

Felix is impressed and feels that there is no case against Paul. But he adjourns the trial for further evidence from Claudius Lysias. (This was only an excuse, for Lysias was never sent for.) He grants Paul reasonable freedom—imprisonment but able to have frequent visitors, Luke, Timothy, Aristarchus, Philip and others. It is believed during this time Luke collected material for his Gospel and, no doubt, for the *Acts*.

What Paul had said made Felix think a good deal. As far as their religion was concerned, the Romans had few if any rites and rules to keep —as had the strict Jews—but they were interested in the gods and anxious to keep on the right side of them! Paul had spoken of his God and a criminal that one of Felix's predecessors had crucified—a certain Jesus. Felix was perplexed. His wife was Drusilla, a young Jewess and daughter of Herod Agrippa I who had murdered James and had himself died a dreadful death at the moment of his vainglory. Paul was sent for and upon being asked, told Felix and Drusilla about his beliefs. Drusilla—who had wrongfully married Felix—saw him as a second John the Baptist who had once accused Herod and his wife Herodias of wickedness. Felix remembered the cruelties of his own rule and his conscience troubled him as he heard Paul speak of his being judged. Paul was dismissed sharply; but note that Felix said he would send for him "at a more convenient season"—or some other time.

Meanwhile, Felix hoped for a bribe, and sent for Paul several times for that reason, believing him to be wealthy enough to produce it. But by his failure to make a decision he missed his real opportunity of believing in Paul's preaching. A short while later Felix was recalled to Rome by Nero, to answer for his cruelties to the Jews. He left Paul in prison to appease the more influential Jews.

Paul and Festus

A year later Paul is still in chains and in prison. There is a new Governor, Festus, whose duty it now is to decide what is to be done with Paul. The Jews of Jerusalem cunningly demand a new trial, in Jerusalem, believing they can hoodwink the new Governor into doing what they want. But Festus is by no means slow to see through this deception and says that if they want a new trial they must come to Caesarea. Reluctantly, they do so. Their charges are, of course, false

A familiar scene in Roman times.   A Centurion leads in his foot-soldiers and their prisoners.

and angry assertions—without proof—that Paul has spoken against the Law (xxv, 8) and against the Temple (xxviii, 19), and against Caesar. Festus, probably bored with the whole affair, but wishing to satisfy the Jews, asks Paul if he is willing to go to Jerusalem for trial. Paul knows perfectly well that this would mean his own death, probably on the journey to the city before he ever got there. He was entitled to justice. He therefore makes his amazing demand. He had long thought about it; it was no decision on the spur of the moment. Despite his chains he would go to Rome where Jesus had said he would one day "bear witness" for Him. He makes his claim as a freeborn citizen—"*I APPEAL UNTO CAESAR*". He would be tried by Nero, in Rome.

Felix consults his legal advisers and then replies, "Unto Caesar then thou shalt go". He is concerned that the business has so far got out of hand and is probably already wondering what

Coins of Emperor Nero, A.D. 54-68.

kind of report he is going to make to Rome. We may be sure that the Jews were furiously angry. Paul had now slipped from their grasp and they could do nothing about it.

Agrippa II

Before sending Paul to Rome, Festus had visitors. King Agrippa II and his sister Bernice came to visit the new Governor now living in the palace where previously their sister Drusilla had held court. Agrippa II was a Jew, ruling under Rome. He had the right to choose the High Priest and had already deposed Ananias. We are told that the priests hated him and had even built a wall in the Temple area to block the view of the king from his palace windows! He came of a line of murderers! His father Agrippa I had murdered James and had sought the life of Peter, too; his great-uncle Herod Antipas had murdered John the Baptist and had taunted Jesus with kingship. His great-grandfather Herod the Great had murdered the babes of Bethlehem. Note that all these evils had been connected in some way with Jesus; and now Festus was to tell Agrippa about Paul who actually believed that this crucified Jesus was still alive! Festus was probably anxious that Agrippa should hear Paul speak, and then advise the Governor how best

In this head of Nero the sculptor has captured the pride of the Roman and the contempt he bore for the Christians.

reminded Agrippa of their common Jewish belief in a Messiah who, said Paul, had indeed come, had been crucified under Pontius Pilate and had risen from the dead. That was over twenty years ago, but he knew that it was true. Jesus had appeared to him on the Damascus road and had sent him to "proclaim light to the people and to the Gentiles". This he had done, first to the Jews, then to the Gentiles, witnessing only what Moses and the prophets had said about the Messiah. For that he had been ill-treated by the Jews. Perhaps anxious that his royal visitors should not be offended, Festus interrupted Paul, who in turn appealed to Agrippa as to the king's belief in the Messiah. Agrippa did not commit himself. He was probably annoyed at being pressed in front of the gathered courtiers and officials. Many people accept his reply, "Almost thou persuadest me to be a Christian", as a cry of willingness to believe. But scholars tell us that the Greek version indicates that it was an answer made in jest. Agrippa, like the Jews of Jerusalem, was too proud and scornful to believe. In Moffatt's translation his words read like a sneer—"At this rate it won't be long before you believe you have made a Christian of me".

Paul's reply was an outburst of sincerity; would that Agrippa and all who heard him might be believers as he, Paul, was—*without the*

to make out his charge sheet and report to Rome. Agrippa was probably curious, since as a Jew he partly sympathised with the Sanhedrin. But he would now be able to listen to Paul, of whom he had heard, and the man's preaching would be a relief from the dullness of a state visit to Caesarea.

Paul and Agrippa

Paul's meeting with Agrippa is sometimes interpreted as another trial. It was not. It was merely an occasion to satisfy Agrippa's interest. Paul did not by any means treat it as a trial. He knew that he could have no further inquiry now that he had demanded to go to Rome. But it was a great opportunity for him to tell his story once more, and this time to a king and to a Jew. Try to picture the scene. The gaily-cloaked Romans, the soldiers in their glittering mail and plumed helmets, trumpeters announcing the king and his sister—who came exquisitely robed and wearing jewels in her hair and on her wrist—"with great pomp". And before them stands a little, dark man, his hair greying, his eyes fiercely bright, burning with zeal that not even the chains on his wrists can withhold.

Paul spoke in cultured, careful Greek. He

A Roman lady.

A Centurion.

Bronze casts of the Roman Gods Cupid and Jupiter.

EXPRESSION WORK

1. Write a dialogue between Ananias the High Priest, and Tertullus the lawyer, in which they prepare a plan of action for the trial of Paul.
2. Re-write Paul's defence in modern language. Declaim it to the class, or use it at a Morning Assembly.
3. Dramatise the trial.
4. *Boys* As Felix, write to Festus in Rome about Paul. *Girls* As Drusilla, write to Bernice in Jerusalem about Paul.
5. What were some of the things Festus would ask Paul on meeting him for the first time? What would Paul tell him?
6. "I appeal unto Caesar." Why was Paul's decision such an important one? Discuss whether or not he was wise to do this.
7. Draw a "family tree" of the Herod family.
8. Draw and colour the scene of Paul before Agrippa.
9. As Festus, write your report on Paul; this will be sent to Nero, and should be a formal document with the correct procedure of greetings, contents and ending.
10. As a Roman, write home about Paul's speech before Agrippa and say what impressed you about the event.
11. Let Agrippa, Festus and Bernice talk (*a*) before, (*b*) after, listening to Paul.
12. Learn 1 John iv, 7–11, 18–21.

chains! Paul must have impressed Agrippa, vaguely irritated though the king may have been. He remarked to Festus that had Paul not appealed to Nero he might have been released straight away. But the appeal to Rome had to be carried out. Festus was still far from clear on what Paul's "crimes" really were, but his report to Rome must have been a favourable one for Paul was probably freed by Nero on his first trial. The report would have made interesting reading had it been preserved with that of Lysias written three years before.

The kind of ship in which Paul left Caesarea on his voyage to Rome. It is described on p. 87. It is easy to see how much it would be at the mercy of strong winds.

CHAPTER 13

THE JOURNEY TO ROME

(xxvii–xxviii, 16)

IT is now August, A.D. 58. You will see by his use of "we" that Luke is with Paul. His eye-witness account is extraordinarily vivid and accurate. Paul is put in the care of Julius, the centurion in charge of one of the corps of soldiers whose special work it was to carry out duties connected with Rome and the armies scattered throughout the Empire. Possibly part of the Praetorian Guard, they acted as couriers and escorts to the more important prisoners; they also had to visit towns and areas and report on the efficiency of the existing forces. This body of men was called the Augustan Band, probably because Augustus Caesar had made it a per-manent corps for these purposes.

The Journey Begins

Sailing in the eastern Mediterranean was dan-gerous after mid-September and the season ended for the winter in November. There would be no ship going across the sea direct to Rome, but there was no time for delay if the company were to get there by winter. They embarked at *Caesarea* in an Adramyttium coaster whose captain touched at harbours along the coast in order to reach safety from sudden storms and high seas. The ship put in at *Sidon*, and Paul was allowed "on parole" to visit his friends. Then the boat continued westwards round the coast of Cilicia. No doubt Paul longed to land and make a brief visit to Tarsus. The prevailing westerly winds drove the boat under the shelter and to the east of Cyprus, the normal route for the time of the year (despite xxvii, 5). Ships of those days carried a mainsail and foresail; they could not tack against a strong wind and had therefore to move under the force of these prevailing winds. Most ships from Alexandria found it easier to sail northwards to Asia Minor and thence in the lee of the coast, rather than north-west to Sicily and Italy. At *Myra*, they changed to a larger government ship making for Puteoli. Here is a fine description by Lucian, a Greek writer, of such a ship:

"What a big ship she is, a hundred and twenty cubits long the shipwright said, and more than a quarter of this in breadth; from deck to bottom there are nine and twenty cubits. And then how huge the mast is, and what a great yard, and what forestays! To see the stern curving up gently like a goose's neck, and the prow stretch-ing out so far, with the image on both sides of Isis after whom the ship is named! Then the decorations, the paintings and the bright-coloured topsail, the anchors and capstans and windlasses and the cabins aft—all this seemed to me completely wonderful. Why, you might compare the number aboard to an army, and enough corn was there, I am told, to feed the whole of Attica for a year."

Julius had the power to take command of the ship. There may have been the full two hundred and seventy-six persons mentioned in the nar-rative, but some MSS. omit the two and give the number as seventy-six. The winds drove the ship from *Cnidus* southwards towards *Crete* and for more secure control it was steered round the north-east point and along the south of the island. This gave them the benefit of shelter in the lee of the mountain range that lay across the island edging the sea in great jagged cliffs. *Salmone* was a promontory jutting eastwards into the sea. They arrived at *Fair Havens* (the present-day name of the harbour) halfway along the coast, and there decided to shelter. During the delay it is possible that Paul visited *Lasea* (xxvii, 7, 8).

A Dangerous Voyage

The rest of the journey was now realised to be extremely dangerous, since they would soon be at the mercy of the winds at a bad time of the

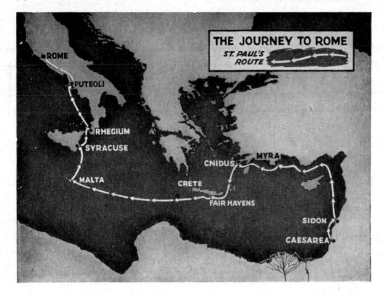

The route taken by the ships on a voyage was determined by the weather at the time of the year. Can you explain this?

year. The reference (9) to the Fast—the Day of Atonement (Book III)—which was held at the end of the Feast of Tabernacles, indicates that it was then early October. It was, therefore, now past the safety period and Paul, at a meeting of the chief officers of the ship and soldiers, warned them of the possible hazards. He knew only too well of the perils of shipwreck (2 Cor. xi, 25). You may wonder why he, a prisoner, was present at such a meeting; perhaps it was because in his conversations with Julius and the ship's captain, Paul had spoken of his travels and knowledge of the sea. In any case, he was an unusual prisoner on his way to see Nero, the Emperor.

Julius wanted to get to Rome and the ship's officers—probably a little jealous of Paul, and also anxious to be with their wives and families—supported the centurion in his decision to continue the journey. They planned to reach Phenice (Phoenix), forty miles farther on.

Here is the ship storm-tossed and doomed. Paul knew what it meant to be shipwrecked and knew when danger threatened.

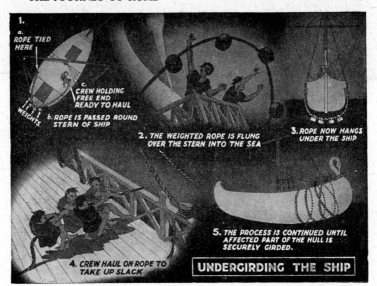

The ship was "undergirded" (xxvii, 17). Why? This pictorial diagram shows how this was done.

Rounding the promontory in a favourable breeze the ship now lost the shelter of the island and was exposed to the full fury of the storm. The powerful and stormy Euraquilo (Euroclydon) blew across Crete, down the frozen slopes of Mount Ida, and caught them unprepared. For twenty miles the ship sped helplessly before the wind until it gained the lee of a tiny island of *Clauda* (Cauda), where they hauled in the water-logged ship's long-boat which had been in tow during the calmer weather a few days before.

Desperate Measures

Passengers, crew and soldiers cleared the deck of gear and tackle. Then they undergirded the ship to ease the strain on the timbers. The drawings show how this was done.

There was a new danger to the south—the quicksands of Syrtis, off the North African coast. The ship, with a small storm-sail, was allowed to drift. The precious cargo of grain was thrown overboard, then the rest of the ship's movable gear, including the heavy mainyard. In the darkness those on board gave themselves up for lost. Without sun or stars they could not have steered even if the storm had abated, for in those days they had no other means of navigation. Like Jesus, Paul found strength in prayer and his

confidence gave the others great courage. After two weeks' drifting in the Sea of Adria, the sailors' name for the eastern Mediterranean, experienced ears caught the sound of breakers dashing on some shore (28). Soundings proved that land was near. Four anchors were dropped from the stern so as to prevent the ship from swinging on to the rocks; then, they "wished for day". What a world of despair and lost hope those words hold.

Shipwrecked

Pretending to attend to the anchors the cowardly sailors lowered the ship's boat in order to escape. But Paul—and we see here his forcefulness of character and practical nature—advised Julius to stop them. He pointed out the need for food, then "took bread", gave thanks, broke it and they all ate. The rest of the cargo serving as ballast was put overboard, and, driven by its mainsail, the ship struck a sandbank stretching between two seas. This is the neck of land still showing across *St. Paul's Bay*, on the northern tip of *Melita*, the island now known as Malta G.C.

Julius, in order to save Paul, ordered the soldiers not to kill their prisoners, although it was their duty to do so to prevent escape. They all reached "safe to land". The inhabitants of

The grain-ship coasted beneath the craggy cliffs of Crete.

their name would appeal to the superstitious; the Roman soldiers felt that such a good sign meant a safe voyage. They touched at *Syracuse* in Sicily, perhaps unloading grain or taking on extra cargo or more passengers; this made three days' delay. Then, on to *Rhegium*, along the "toe" of Italy; Vesuvius, belching smoke over the unsuspecting city of Pompeii at its foot, came into view as a favourable wind drove them along the west coast of Italy, to *Puteoli* (Pozzuoli). This was a large trading port, 140 miles from Rome. The grain-ship proudly entered with her topsails set—an honour to which she was entitled. There was a Christian community here, which is not surprising at such a trading centre. Tradition says that Peter had already been in Rome since A.D. 42 and that he had founded a church at Puteoli. Paul and Luke stayed here with friends for seven days.

Malta were non-Greeks of Phoenician origin; Luke calls them "barbarians", but they were kindly people, preparing a fire and food for the shipwrecked company. They regarded Paul as a criminal when the snake clung to him; then they thought he must be a god. Publius gave Paul and the chief officers hospitality for three days, during which time Paul and Luke healed and tended many sick people including the father of Publius.

Forty miles from Rome, along the Appian Way, was *Appii Forum* (market of Appius). All roads led to Rome; this one was from Brindisi and like all of them was measured from the Golden Milestone in the centre of the Imperial City. It was but one of the many Paul had traversed. His Good News had passed along many of them and would go out and along them to the whole world. Christians now came as far as this to greet Paul with a great welcome. They travelled another ten miles to *The Three Taverns*, where for years men had found a forge, a store and a place to drink. Here, more Christians joined them.

And So to Rome

It was now about February, A.D. 59, and although much before the safe sailing period began, Julius decided to take advantage of the presence of another ship from Alexandria which had wintered in the island. This was the "Twin Brothers", named after Castor and Pollux. These were the gods of sailors and a ship with

Thus welcomed, Paul "took courage". The strain of the voyage had taken toll of his energy and spirit; the malarial effect of the Pontine

This is St. Paul's Bay, the traditional place of the shipwreck. On the island on the right is a statue of Paul.

Part of the famous Roman Appian Way (Via Appia), a paved military highway to Brindisi linking Rome with the Adriatic and beyond.

Marshes made him weak and listless. But now he was with friends and in sight of his goal. He was uplifted and strengthened. In this great joy and greater relief he arrived at the gates of *Rome*.

Rome

It was A.D. 59. This was Rome, the Imperial City, "Mistress of the World", wicked, wealthy, Godless. From the hill-top Paul could see the aqueduct of Claudia and the Pyramid of Caius Cestius, the Capitol, the Palace and the Senate House. There were triumphal arches commemorating past victories and campaigns. There were hundreds of shrines and temples to dozens of gods and goddesses—to Romulus, Vesta, Serapis, Isis, Mithras. Luke would note a temple to the god of medicine, Aesculapius. There lay the Forum and the huge Circus Maximus where thousands of slaves and, later, Christians, were murdered by wild animals. Some of Paul's companions would be sacrificed in that very arena to amuse the watching crowds. That was where the great fire was to begin in A.D. 64 from which Nero would take his excuse to persecute the Christians. The Colosseum where Ignatius of Antioch was to die was yet to be built—five years after Paul's own death—by twelve thousand Jews sent in chains to Rome, after the sack of Jerusalem by Titus, son of the Emperor Vespasian, in A.D. 70.

Paul had said he would see Rome; and now he was there. Julius handed him—chained by his right hand to his Roman guard's left—to the officer in charge of the camp on the Coelian Hill just outside the city walls. This guard was part of the special corps of which Julius was centurion —the Imperial Couriers.

Paul Meets the Jews

For two years Paul was to live a shackled

The last stages of Paul's journey to Rome.

This is how Paul may have entered Rome, chained and a prisoner.

prisoner "on bail" in a house rented at his own expense. Three days after arriving, unable to attend the synagogue, he called a meeting of the elders of the Jewish synagogue. He gave them a brief summary of his experiences and why he had come to Rome. The Jews appeared to be somewhat unfriendly. To them, he was a strict Jew who had denied his upbringing to preach belief in a crucified Messiah. They had no knowledge of his appeal to Caesar and their idea of Christianity was that it was not a very highly thought of religion but one which they had heard of as everywhere "spoken against". They accepted the fact that Paul was the leader of the new sect and asked to hear more about it. He promised to explain his Good News. They came again and he did so, but they were divided in their opinions. Paul remembered his scriptures. The quotation he made (26, 27) is from Isa. vi, 9, 10—from the LXX. His decisive point was that "salvation of God is sent unto the Gentiles". The Jews of Rome could not accept this—"they

The Colosseum is now in ruins. Once it echoed to the screams of victims, the roars of lions, the shouts and cheers of onlookers.

agreed not among themselves"—and Paul knew that the old opposition of the Jews was once more against him. But he continued to preach to all who wanted to listen to him.

Luke's story ends here and the rest of our information is obtained from Paul's epistles and traditional legends. There may have been a third book by Luke, but we have no trace of it. But this was not the end of Paul, nor of his work. The message of Christianity had at last reached the heart of the Empire from which it must spread throughout the whole world.

EXPRESSION WORK

1. Keep a daily "log" of the voyage to Rome.
2. Draw and colour or prepare on scraper-board, the ship or the wreck on Malta.
3. Debate the advisability of continuing the voyage. The group should include Paul, Julius, the ship's captain and others.
4. Study closely the drawings that show how the ship was "undergirded". Describe it.
5. As passengers and members of the crew, talk together about the voyage and its dangers. Now let Paul join you and react to his advice and confidence.
6. Make a verbal report that an islander might take to Publius on seeing or hearing about the wreck.
7. Learn for Choral Verse-speaking Rom. viii, 31–39; xii, 9–21. Letter for display viii, 28.
8. Describe a visit to Rome in A.D. 59.
9. Dramatise Paul's first meeting with the Jews in Rome.
10. Prepare a dialogue between Peter and Paul.
11. Write a report such as Julius might have submitted to Nero.
12. In "Songs of Praise" or some other hymn-book, find the tune "Melita". What is the hymn for which it was written? Is it a suitable name for this tune? Use the hymn in a Service on the theme "Our Sailors" or "For Those at Sea". Psalm cvii, 23–30, could be your reading. Why?

★   ★   ★

In the huge arena chariots hurtled in furiously-fought races to thrill the spectators packed on either side.

CHAPTER 14

"THROUGHOUT ALL THE WORLD"

DURING the two years that Paul was held, he preached freely. Phil. i, 12; iv, 22, indicate that much good work was done with his guards. This is not surprising, for to be chained to a man like Paul was indeed the first step to being converted to his faith.

Paul's Letters

Luke was still with him and, for a time, Timothy. There was John Mark, too, now forgiven by Paul and a likely young preacher. Whilst a prisoner Paul wrote several letters to friends and churches. One of these is the only private letter we have, sent to a Christian friend in Colossae. It is about a slave. In many cities four out of every five people were slaves. Rome had twice as many slaves as free citizens. Life for a slave was short and held cheap; no one cared for him. But a runaway slave, Onesimus by name, comes to Rome. He has probably robbed his master and seeks in Rome adventure and fortune. Having no doubt heard his master speak of Paul, Onesimus goes to him and after a while admits what he has done. Paul has grown to love the lad but knows it is his duty to send him back to his master. As a slave Onesimus could be brutally but lawfully beaten, even to death. Paul therefore writes to *Philemon*, telling him that Onesimus is to be "redeemed", i.e. given his freedom, and that he is to be adopted as his "brother in Christ". Philemon owes this to Paul (verse 19. Cf. Col. iii, 22,–iv, 1). Greatly trusting, Paul hands the letter to Onesimus to deliver by hand to his master. We can only guess at what happened, but knowing Paul and remembering that the name of Onesimus means "worth", we may feel that the slave found in his master a Christian brother. There is a tradition that Onesimus became a bishop. It is worth noting that some scholars think Paul wrote this letter when imprisoned at Ephesus, not far from Colossae. If so, Onesimus sought adventure in Ephesus, not Rome.

The "Plan" of Paul's Letters

Like most eastern writers, Paul usually followed a set plan in his letters, which were written, of course, on papyrus (Book I). In the letter to Philemon you will see that verses 1–3 form the greeting; 4–7 contain thanksgiving and prayer; 8–22 are the main contents of the letter; 23–25 convey a greeting and benediction or blessing. This was the form or style of the time and is to be found in letters by writers other than Paul. The scribe often adds his own message, e.g. Rom. xvi, 22, and Paul occasionally "autographs" his letter—1 Cor. xvi, 21; Gal. vi, 11; 2 Thess. iii, 17. This signature was appreciated by those who received the letter, as it was a special mark of favour to write a letter in one's own hand.

Scholars who have studied the Greek language tell us that he wrote in the same colloquial speech of the "man in the street" that he used in his preaching. This meant that wherever they came from people could understand his message. Translated into the beautiful Elizabethan English of the A.V. of our Bible, Paul's letters are often difficult to follow, not only because they often deal with problems of which we know nothing but also because not always the best and most exact words were used in this version. It is important to use a modern translation when studying Paul's letters, in order to appreciate how straightforward and "modern" his letters really are. One thing is certain. Paul could never have dreamed that his letters would be read nineteen hundred years later by people all over the world in hundreds of different languages.

To the Colossians and Ephesians

Another visitor at this time was Epaphras, one of the chief members of the church at Colossae,

Inside the Colosseum in Rome. Christians were thrown to the lions because they would not give up their belief in Jesus. Today it is in ruins, but the Christian faith lives on.

a hundred miles east of Ephesus, whose church members had begun it. His problem was that a new preacher was bringing strange ideas into the Christian church. Although he had never been there, Paul was asked to help. He wrote his letter and his friend Tychicus took it. Paul advised the Colossians on what the Christian faith really was and asked them to practise the Christian virtues, to be kind, forgiving and forbearing. Tychicus accompanied Onesimus on his way home to Philemon (Col. iv, 7–9).

In this letter Paul refers to a similar one written to the church in Laodicea (Col. iv, 16; cf. Rev. i, 11; iii, 14). He tells them to exchange their letters. It seems that this particular one was more of a "circular" letter outlining Christian life and behaviour. It is possible that this is the letter today called the Epistle to the *Ephesians* because it is the only copy of the letter existing. It lacks the friendly touches one would expect from Paul to friends in the city (cf. Eph. iii, 2) and who had journeyed to Miletus to bid him a last farewell. Yet this letter is probably the finest of all Paul's epistles. It is inspired and noble. Paul says that even before the coming of Jesus God's plan was to rid mankind of evil; Jesus was sent to do this and to bring all men everywhere back to Him. This was to be done through the Church of Christ, His Kingdom on earth (Eph. ii, 12–20; iii, 11; iv, 1–6, 17, 22–25, 28–32; v, 1, 2, 8, 11, 21–25; vi, 5, 6, 9). Therefore, says Paul, they should behave worthily of this great calling and form a united church.

With his eye on the burly Roman guard to whom he was chained Paul wrote words that have become memorable to us all; you can read them in Eph. vi, 10–18.

Epistle to the Philippians

On one occasion Paul was visited by Epaphroditus who had brought gifts from Philippi. His friend became ill and when he had recovered Paul decided to send by him a letter to his friends in the city—the jailer, Lydia and others. It was a happy letter, full of joy, written in the desire to cheer the Christians who had been anxious about him and to urge fellowship and sharing (Phil. iv, 1, 4, 10). In iv, 8, we have some of the most beautiful words in the whole Bible. His many friends included the servants of Caesar's household, who sent their greetings.

Paul speaks of several imprisonments and nothing is certain about the "captivity epistles" as they are called—*Ephesians, Colossians, Philemon* and *Philippians*. They may have come from Caesarea, or Ephesus, but it is generally accepted that they were written from Rome.

Like other emperors, Constantine raised his arch of victory.

Roman Suspicion

Meanwhile, in Rome, there was already unrest in the Emperor's Court. The Emperor himself held highest place in their worship, for he had been accepted as a god since the days of Octavius. There were "mystery" religions with magical rites and strange forms of ritual that attracted the common people; there were religions based on philosophy that tried to "explain" life to people; there were different beliefs in gods from other lands—Cybele from Phrygia, Isis

The Temple of Vesta the fire of which was never allowed to die out.

from Egypt and Mithras from Persia. The worship of Mithras was the strongest of all and, for years, even in England, was a rival to Christianity. It offered a belief in an after-life and drew soldiers especially to its temples.

But Christianity offered all the good things the other religions had—freedom, life hereafter, and a *real* God and Saviour.

Until now, the Christians had been regarded tolerantly, so long as their beliefs did not challenge law and order or the power of Caesar. But these Christians were now refusing to burn incense at the statue of Nero or to join in pagan festivals and processions. They held "secret meetings" of their own members and shared a secret meal. They were beginning to talk of their Messiah Christ as a great God and Saviour—words previously used by the Romans to describe their own emperors. Julius Caesar had been hailed as "God made manifest . . . the Saviour of human life". Augustus Caesar was called "God of God" . . . and "Son of God". He and Claudius were even called "God and Lord". Nero was now being called "Lord" (xxv, 26) and "Emperor-God". Their royal decrees were described as "Holy Scriptures".

It was natural that in their worship of the emperor-god the Romans should view with suspicion any one who not only refused to acknowledge the emperor as god—which Christians could not do without denying God—but who also described their own God with the very words—Lord, Saviour, Divine God—used for the Roman Caesars.

Rome became antagonistic and resolved to take a firmer hold upon these obstinate Christians. There is no doubt, of course, that, pagan as they were, the Romans did realise that the new way of life of these people offered rest and joy and a better life. But they deliberately rejected it and became not only suspicious but also hostile. It needed but one incident to begin open persecution, and once it started in the capital city it would flare through the whole Roman Empire in an effort to stamp out this Christian religion. It was becoming unsafe even then to admit publicly that one was a Christian.

The one incident came in A.D. 64—the Fire of Rome. Eager to find a scapegoat Nero put the blame upon the Christians, and so began the

One of the chief attractions in a gladiatorial show was the duel between man and beast. One or other had to die before the crowd was satisfied.

dreadful persecutions whose awful stories have come down to us through history. Christians were tortured, crucified, sewn into the skins of animals and put before wild beasts in the arenas; some were even covered in tar and burnt alive as human torches to light up the emperor's gardens whilst he and his friends feasted and drank.

What Happened to Paul?

Where was Paul at this time? It is generally believed that at the end of two years he had been released by Nero, probably because of the favourable reports of Festus and Julius and possibly Agrippa. We are told that according to Roman law no prisoner could be kept beyond eighteen months if no charge was made against him. The Jews in Jerusalem seem not to have followed up their original charges and the Romans had none to make, so Paul was probably freed after the eighteen months, i.e. "about" two years.

In about A.D. 61, therefore, he was free to travel once again, preaching the "Lord Jesus Christ" and establishing more firmly the Christian faith. He may have visited Philemon in Colossae as he had promised in his letter. Tradition says he went as far as Spain. At the time of the persecutions he was far from Rome, somewhere in Asia Minor, and possibly at Ephesus. He would be watched and any one of his enemies would betray him. In 2 Tim, iv, 14, he refers to the accusations of "Alexander the coppersmith"; it may have been he who gave away his whereabouts, somewhere near Troas, for Paul was at last arrested. On his right of appeal to Caesar he was brought back to Rome, his only companion the faithful Luke. Legend says that he was thrown into prison with Peter. He was closely guarded, no longer able to see his friends. Most of them had fled. "They have all turned away from me," he wrote.

The "Pastoral Letters"

It was whilst he was in prison at this time that Paul may have written his three letters to encourage Timothy and Titus. They are full of wise advice on Christian conduct and encouragement in their work as church leaders. A minister today is called a "pastor", hence these letters are called "pastoral letters". Scholars tell us that only fragments of the letters are really by Paul, but we can sense the words that only Paul could have written.

Titus had been put in charge of the Christian Church in Crete. Later, Paul had visited him but not for a long enough stay to do all he wished. As Titus was very young, some of the older members did not want to obey him. Paul therefore wrote to instruct him in church matters and gave him similar advice to that he gave to Timothy.

Paul saw the Pyramid of Cestius on his way to execution.

Timothy was now Bishop of the Church at Ephesus; the word "bishop" really means "president" or even "overseer". Timothy was well-qualified for this honour for he was "well grounded in the scriptures" and had been trained by Paul himself. For his personal guidance see 1 Tim. vi, 11–16. The letters breathe throughout Paul's great love for his "beloved son in the faith", warning him to beware of false teachers and false doctrines. If the first letter was written when Paul was in Macedonia—as is sometimes believed—the second certainly was sent from

prison in Rome. Paul is now an old man, doomed to die for his faith and longing to see Timothy once more before the end (2 Tim. i, 4; iv, 9, 21). The letter is again full of wise counsel, just in case Timothy does not arrive in time. He asks him to bring his tough Cilician cloak to keep him warm in the cold cell—and the books, his scrolls and parchments—"especially the parchments". In iv, 6–8, are written Paul's unforgettable words of triumph and certainty in his faith in Jesus.

Paul is Executed

Paul's trial, like that of any Christian of this time, was without hope. He was the chief of the Christians and must certainly die. Thousands of them had been massacred by fire, sword, torture, thrown to the lions, crucified in the Circus. Paul, to the end, found that his Roman citizenship served him, for he was spared all these things. He was to die a Roman's death—by the sword. Tradition says that he and Peter went out to die together, Peter to the Circus, Paul to the Salvian Springs, a pine wood three miles outside the city. This spot was by the same Pyramid of Cestius that he had seen when he first arrived; it was near the long Roman road that ran to the harbour of Ostia. Perhaps Julius and some of Paul's personal Roman guards watched sadly as the old man, then nearly seventy, knelt for the last time—at the executioner's block. We do not know the exact date, but it was about A.D. 64.

Christianity Comes to England

All through the story of Paul England was being invaded and settled by Roman soldiers at this time. Roman armies had landed in the south and from London (Londinium) had moved across England westwards, eastwards and to the north. Wherever they went they defeated the Britons and set up their own villages and towns —Verulamium, Caerleon, Camalodunum, Eboracum and dozens of others remembered in our history. The Roman soldiers who had worshipped Mithras brought with them their statues of him and set up their shrines. He was an ancient god even in the days of the Persians. Even today there are excavations at Erech in Mesopotamia (Gen. x, 8–10) revealing his temple dated 3,000

In Rome stands the great St. Peter's Church.

In London is St. Paul's Cathedral. Like St. Peter's it is world famous, reminding us of the faith and work of the early followers of Christ.

B.C. Mithras had been taken over by the Romans (Book II, p. 84) and was one of the few Roman gods that offered any kind of immortality and after-life. But amongst these same soldiers were many who had heard of the new Christian faith and had been converted to it. Some of them remained faithful to Mithras but also worshipped Jesus. They knew of Paul and may even have been, at some time, his guards. They knew of the wonderful bravery of the Christians who had died for their faith in the belief that with Jesus they would "rise again". This certainty had made a deep impression upon them and they felt that here was a religion they could accept. It was finer even than that of Mithras.

So it was that Romans and Britons alike grew in the Christian faith, so that when missionaries at last came to England to preach they found many Christians already serving Jesus as Paul had taught that they should.

Some lived their lives around the hill north of the marshy Thames. There they built a temple to Mithras. But they met, too, to worship the Lord of all, and years later, on that hill, there was built the most famous cathedral in the land —perhaps in the whole world—the Cathedral of Saint Paul. The Mithras temple has been discovered and will be preserved as a relic of past centuries, its religion dead. St. Paul's stands today as a reminder of the great missionary Paul and his work in carrying to the "uttermost parts" of the world, Christianity—the faith by which men live!

EXPRESSION WORK

1. Seneca was Gallio's brother and also Prime Minister to Nero. Dramatise the first trial of Paul before Caesar, using information sent by Gallio from Corinth, together with the reports of Festus, Lysias and Agrippa. A report from Julius would also help. There is no accusation from Jerusalem.

2. Draw Paul in prison, guarded by a Roman soldier.

3. As Epaphras discuss the problem of the Colossian church with Paul. As Epaphroditus bring your message and gifts from Philippi.

4. Find all you can about Roman worship. Why was the worship of Mithras "a rival to Christianity"?

This Roman temple to Mithras—the soldier's god—has been found in London. It dates from the 2nd Century A.D.

5. Bring to Nero the report of outbreak of fire in the Circus Maximus area where live most of the Christians. Describe the fire (Rev. xviii. 11–19, may help you to picture it).

6. Learn Eph. iv, 25–32; Phil. iv, 8. Letter 2 Tim. iv, 7.
7. Write and act the meeting of Onesimus and Philemon.
8. Choose twelve Christian martyrs in chronological order. Find all you can about them and give talks to the class about them.
9. As Mark, bring home the news of the deaths of Peter and Paul,
   or
   As Julius, describe to friends in Caesarea how Paul met his death.
10. Divide yourselves into groups of Romans and Britons. Talk about the "new faith" brought to Britain by the Roman soldiers and settlers.
11. Dr. Albert Schweitzer has been called "the Paul of the 20th Century". Find out more about this great man and say if you agree. Is it a compliment to be described in this way? How far is Schweitzer's work like that of Paul? How does it differ?
12. Prepare for Morning Assembly a Service on the theme of "Missionaries" or "Christianity comes to England",
   or
   Look up the following references and write down the sentences that strike you as wise sayings. Find out what they mean: 1 Cor. xv, 33; 2 Cor. ix, 7; Gal. v, 9; Gal. vi, 7; Gal. vi, 9; 1 Tim. v, 18; 1 Tim. vi, 10; Titus i, 15.

On the base of an early Christian drinking-cup found in the Catacombs is this etching. Peter and Paul receive "crowns of righteousness" from their Master.